Horned & Antlered Animals

Horned & Antlered Animals

**Paintings & Monotypes
by Valentina DuBasky**

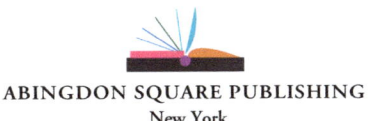

ABINGDON SQUARE PUBLISHING
New York

Copyright © 2020 by Valentina DuBasky

All rights reserved. No part of this publication may be reproduced in any manner, stored in a retrieval system, or transmitted in any form by any means—electronic, mechanical, photocopying, recording or otherwise—without written permission from the publisher, except in article reviews.

Artwork © 2020 by Valentina DuBasky

Horned & Antlered Animals
published by
Abingdon Square Publishing
463 West Street, Suite G122
New York, NY 10014
USA
www.abingdonsquarepublishing.com
Book design: Abingdon Square Publishing

ISBN: 978-1-7349849-0-3
Library of Congress Control Number: 2020945755

Printed in the United States of America

Front Cover: *White Bison with Ochre Markings,* 2020, Oil on canvas, 12 x 16 inches
Back Cover: *Himalayan Antelope with Spiral Horns,* 2019, Oil on canvas, 14 x 11 inches

Table of Contents

Artist's Statement 1
Paintings 3
Monotypes 57

Artist's Statement

The brightly colored paintings and monotypes of bison, goats, stags and antelope in this collection celebrate the shapes and structure of horns and antlers—the spiraling and coiling horns of goats and sheep, the smooth horns of cattle, the meandering or lyre-shaped horns of antelope, and the regal crowns of stags—paired, branched or forked.

The paintings in *Horned and Antlered Animals* are my response to the travels I made on the Silk Routes in China, Central and Southeast Asia, and in India, as a Fulbright Senior Specialist, where opportunities to research Buddhist cave paintings and ancient art provided new inspiration for the work. In India, I was immersed in a world of spectacular colors out of which emerged a new color palette: yellows of marigold, tints of coral, tangerine, mango, flame-orange, ochre, aubergine and sienna, the fullest range of blues, greens, violets and all the compliments.

In the horned and antlered animal paintings I explore the relationship between ancient art and the contemporary imagination through thick impasto paint, incised lines and expressive brushwork. Pitched on the edge of abstraction, the images may be read as animal, abstraction, landscape or still life. Each painting begins with a rectangle that I bisect or divide into areas of color to activate the balance of forms, the relationships of color and the behavior of the materials. Imagination and materials lead the way. The image is present and absent at the same time.

Images of horned and antlered animals, found in abundance throughout the ancient world, have been a sounding board for creative possibilities. The mysterious, shamanic deer stones of Mongolia depict deer that appear to be flying through the air. Incised in stone, the deer defy both the gravity of earth and the weight of stone with their raised heads and outstretched legs. Their antlers, designed with ornate spiraling lines, migrate across the entire length of their backs. Thousands of miles to the west, nomadic people created similar images of golden stags with spiraling horns. In Greek mythology, the story of the Argonauts and the quest for the Golden Fleece features a winged ram that carries Phrixus to Colchis, a region near the Black Sea where archaeologists have unearthed spiral-horned, flying rams made of gold.

I am fascinated by the large charismatic quadrupeds that live in wild, natural places. White face markings, chest patches, blazes, tail tips, and an infinite variety of spots, dappled coats and brindled patterns inspire me to respond through paint.

Valentina DuBasky
New York, NY, 2020

Paintings

White Addax with Magenta Horns, 2020
Oil on canvas, 11 x 14 inches

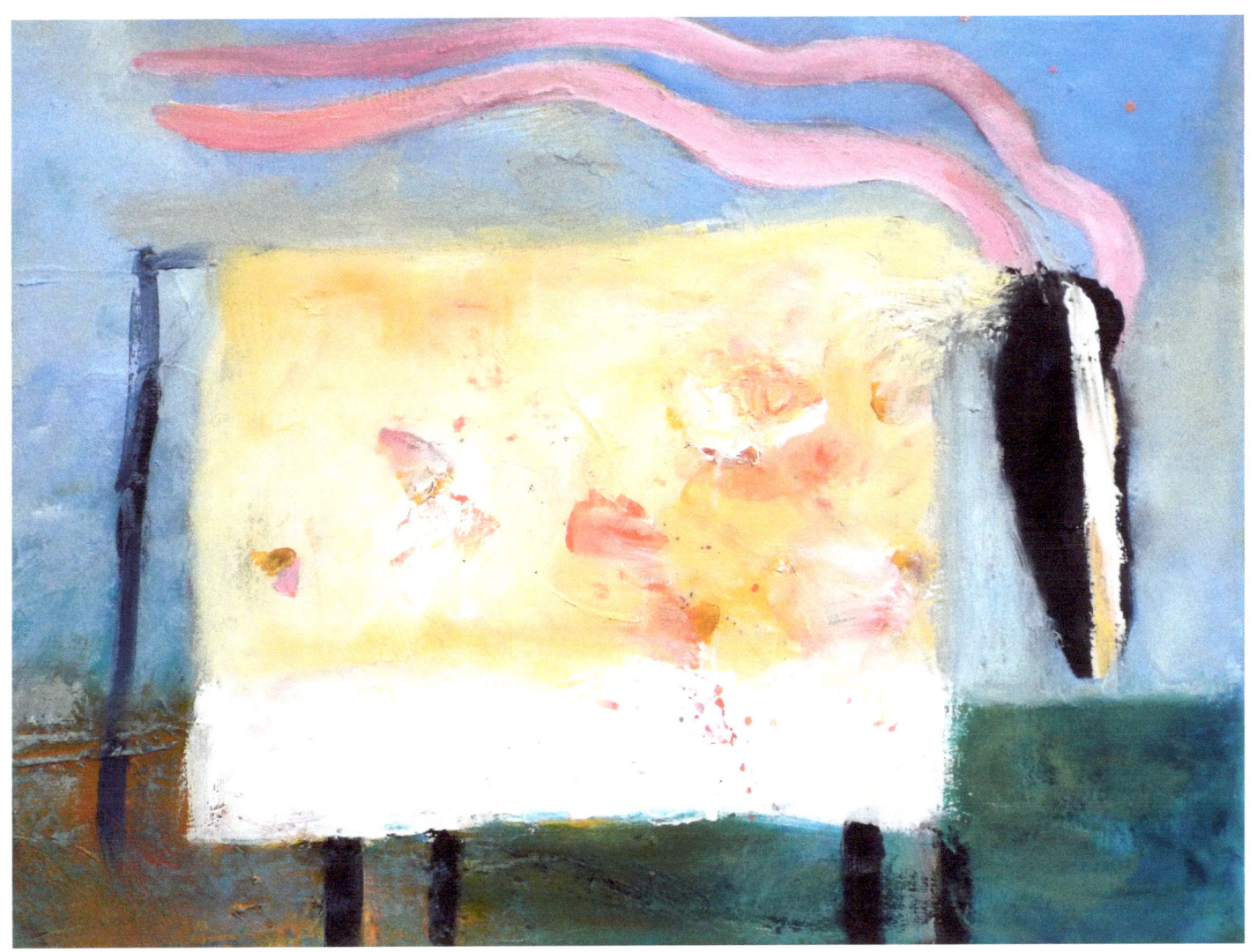

Spotted Goat, 2020
Oil on canvas, 11 x 14 inches

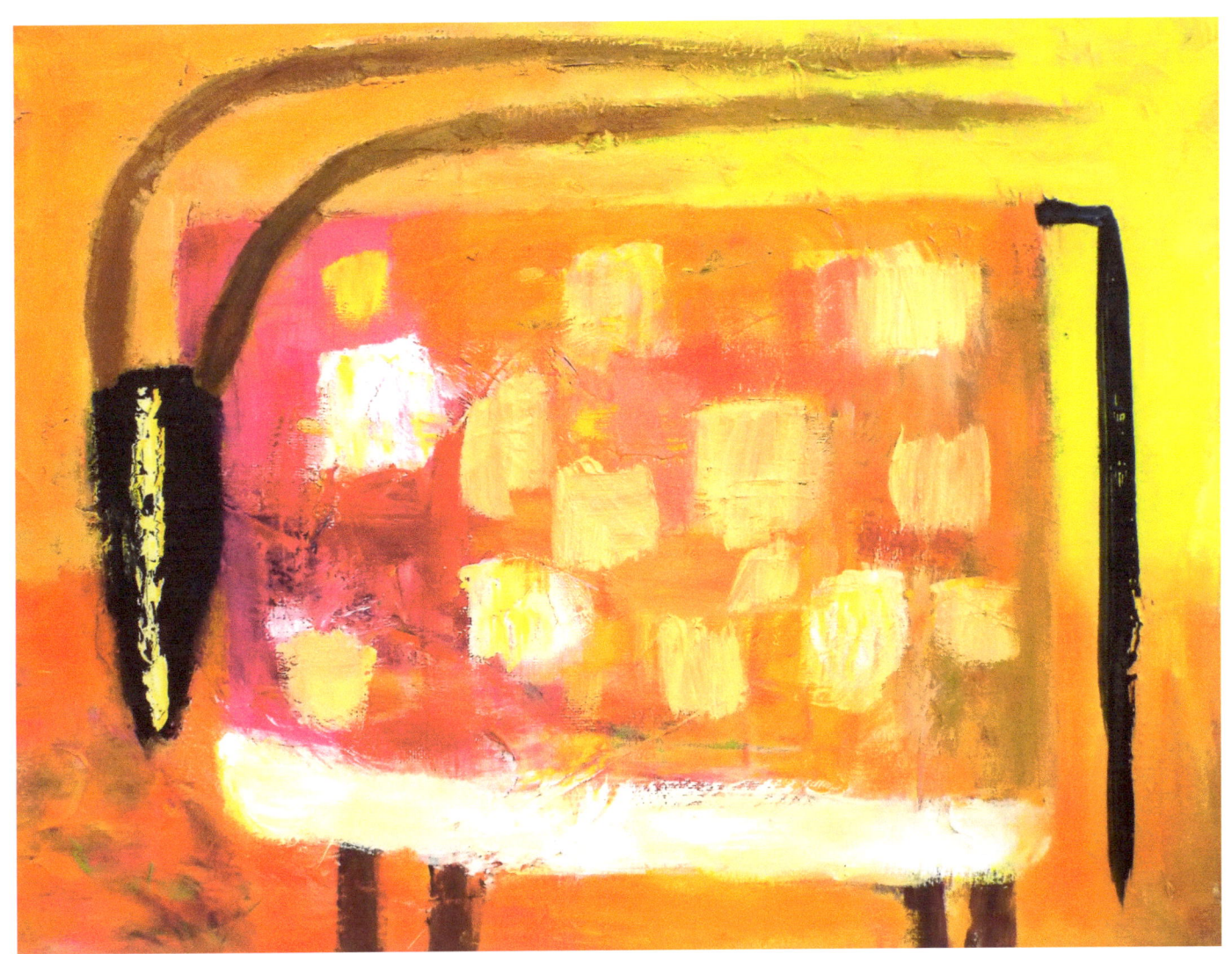

Markhor, 2020
Oil on paper, 20 x 24 inches

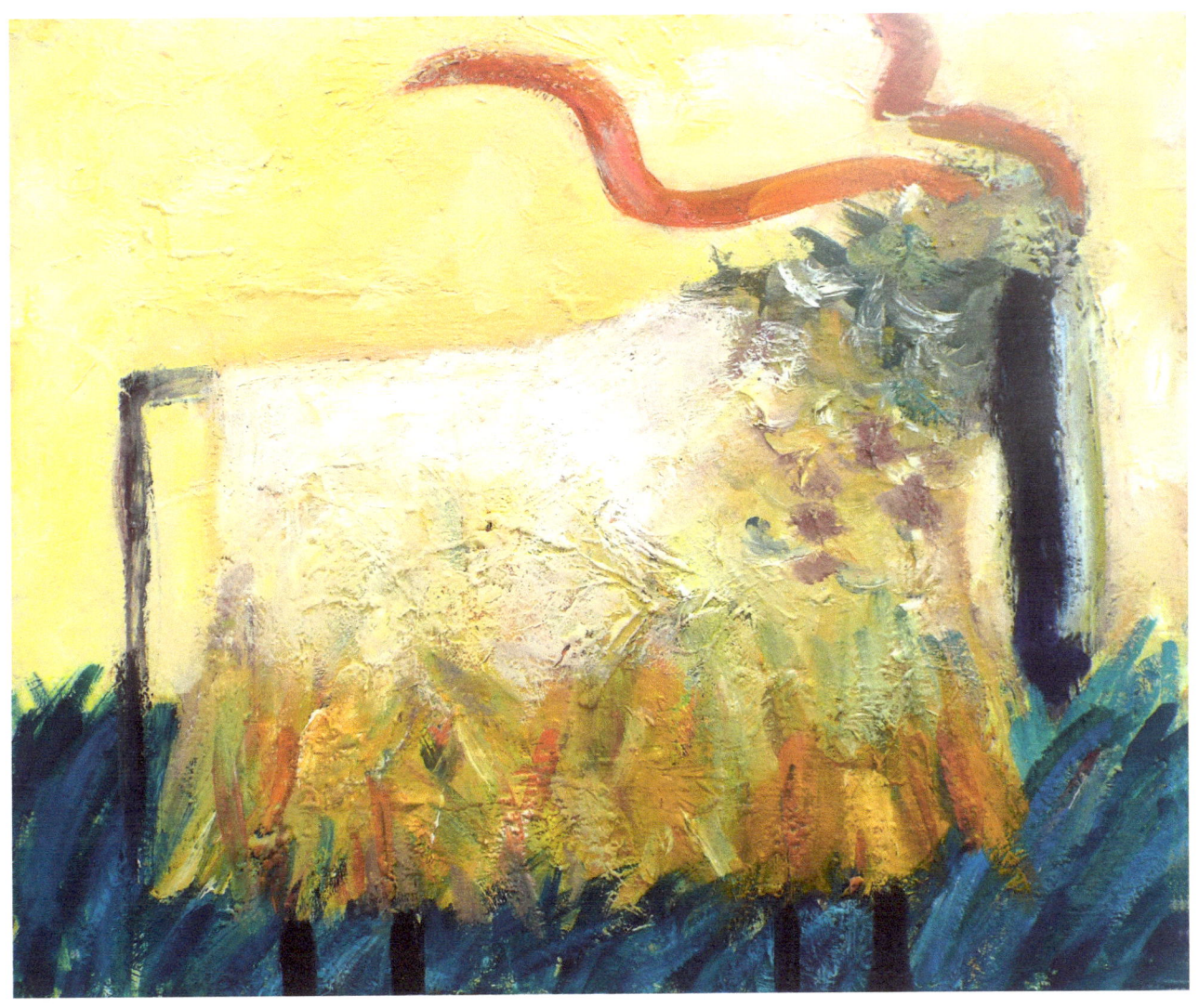

Spotted Goat in Red Field, 2018
Oil on canvas, 22 x 30 inches

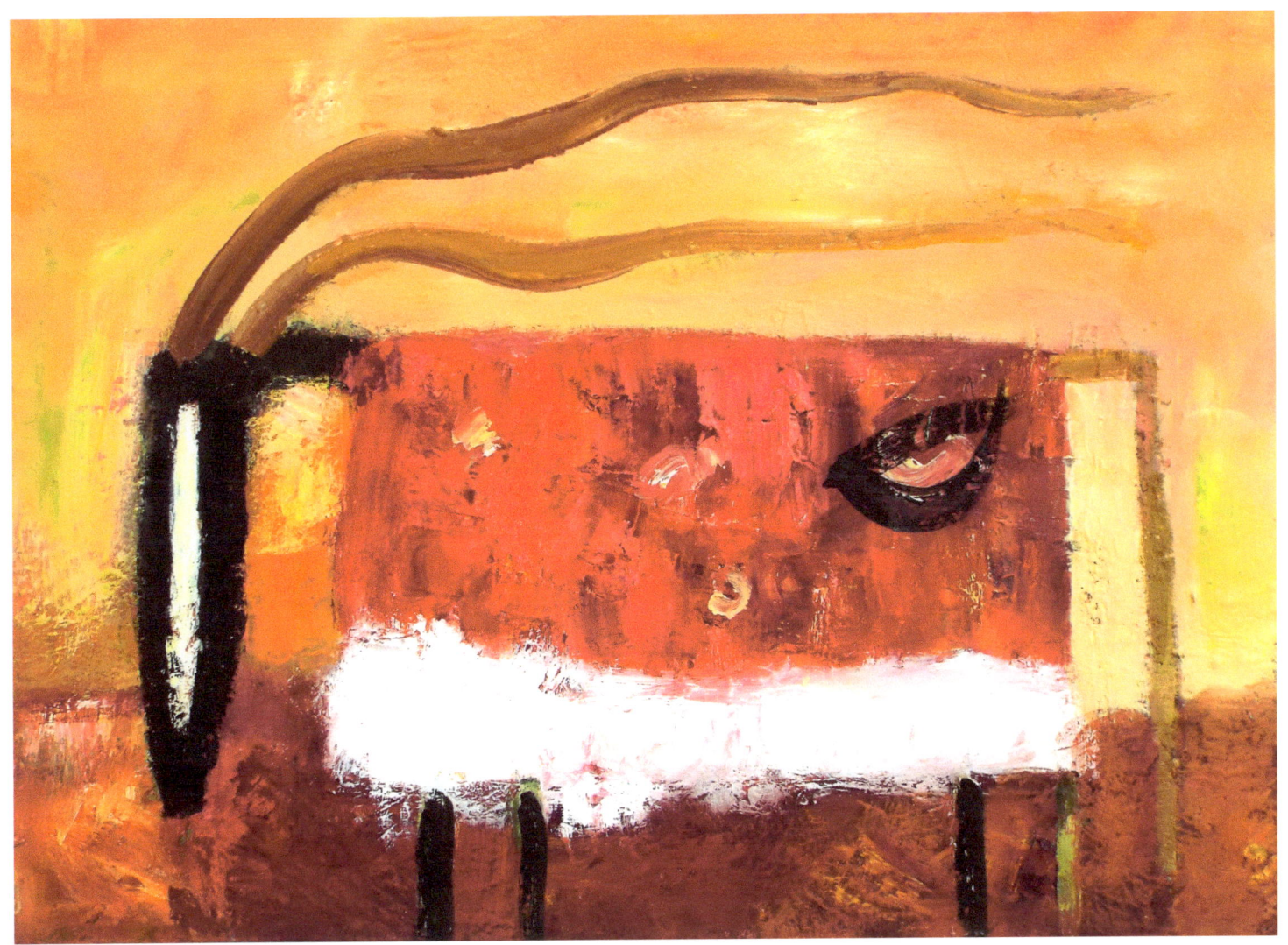

Himalayan Antelope with Spiral Horns, 2019
Oil on canvas, 14 x 11 inches

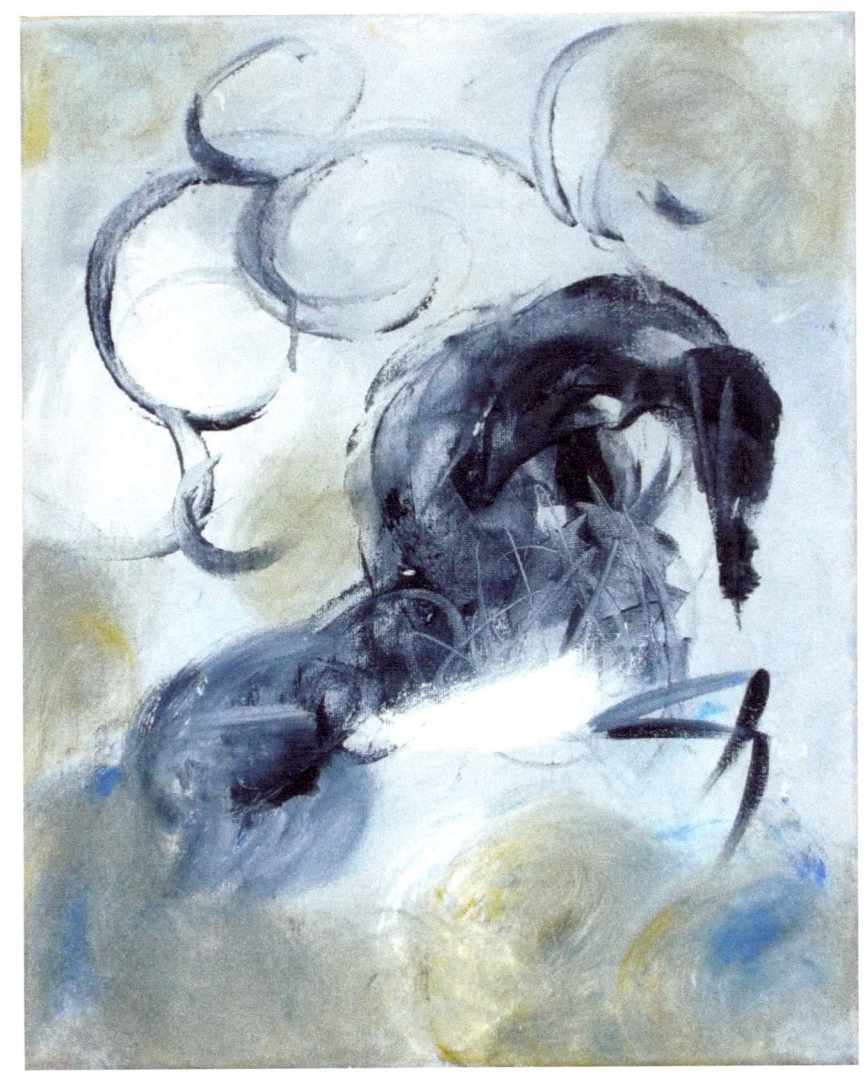

White Ram with Spiral Horns, 2020
Oil on canvas, 14 x 11 inches

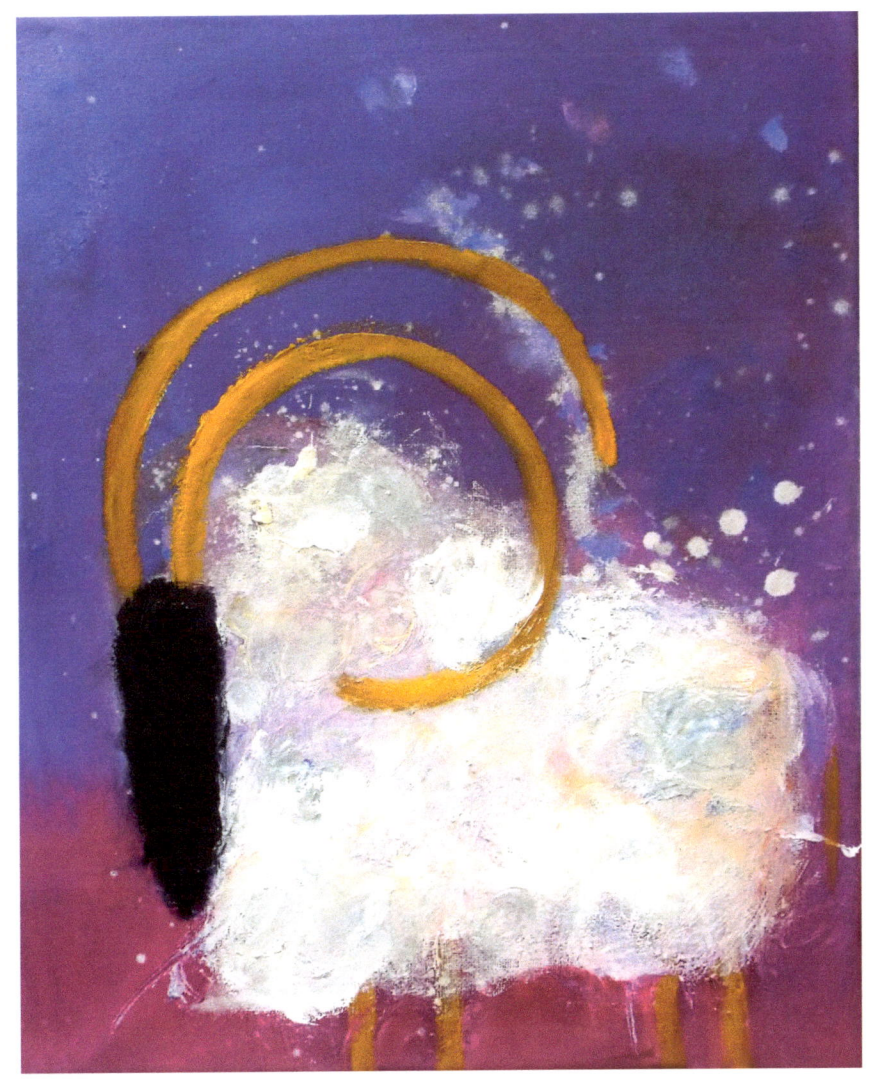

Recumbent Bull with Blue Horns, 2020
Oil on canvas, 14 x 11 inches

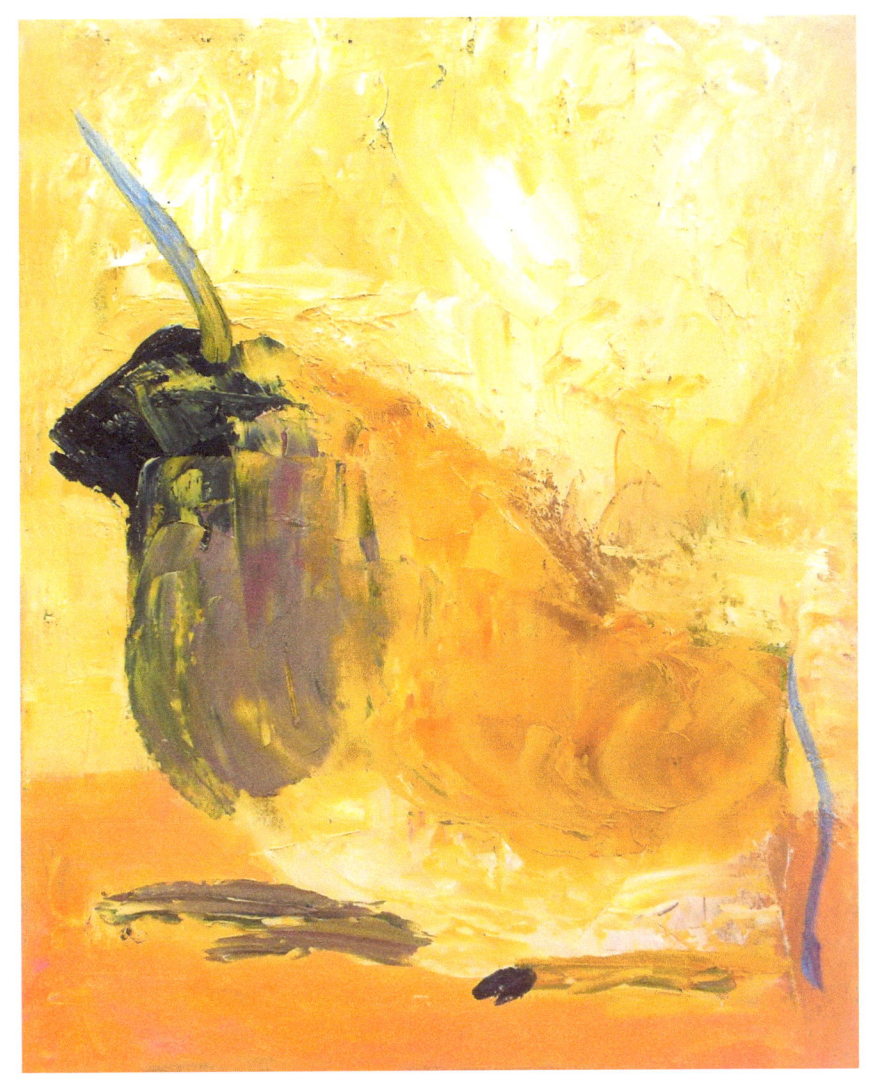

Bison, 2017
Acrylic on plaster and paper, 30.5 x 33 inches

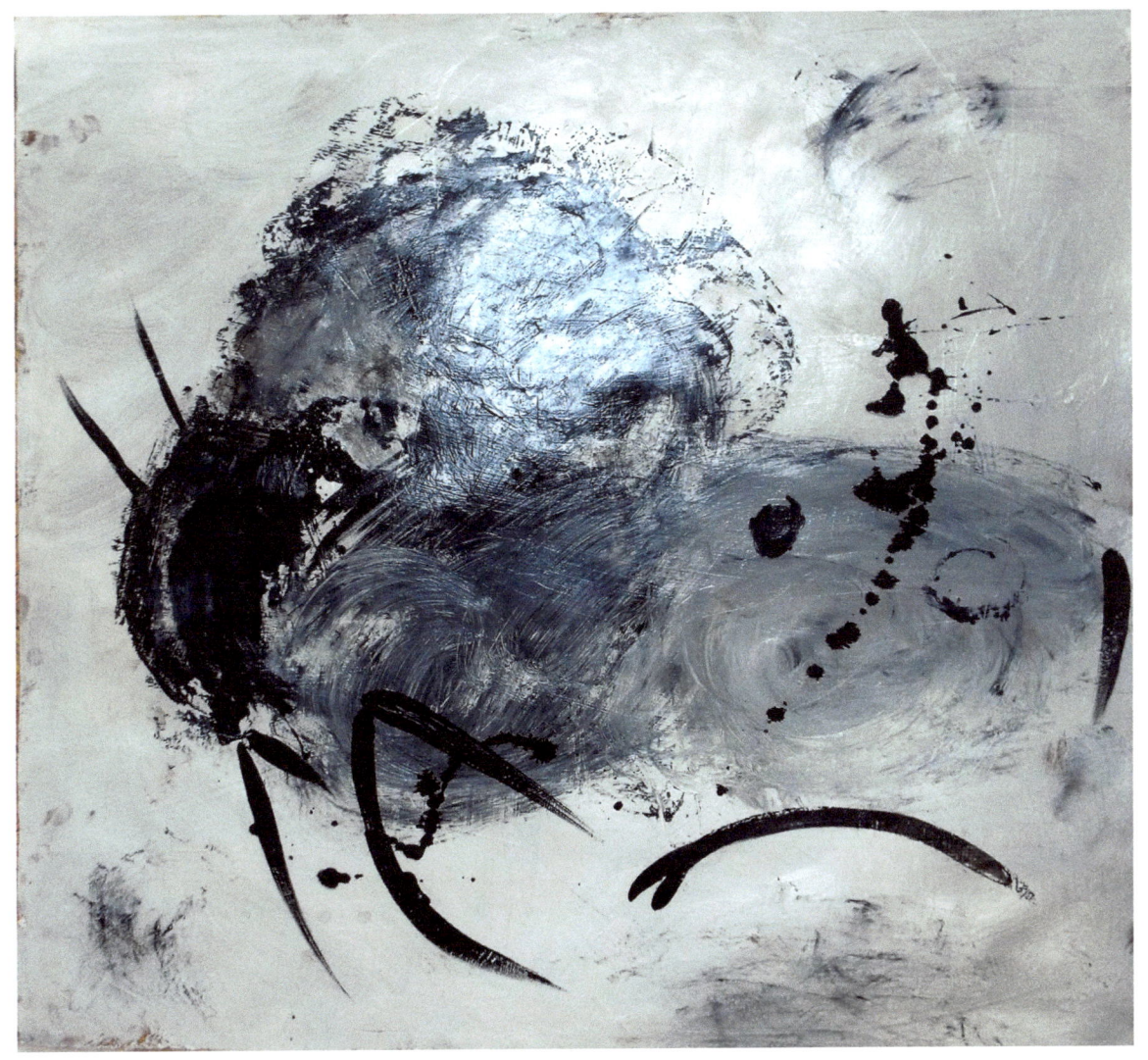

White Bison with Ochre Markings, 2020
Oil on canvas, 12 x 16 inches

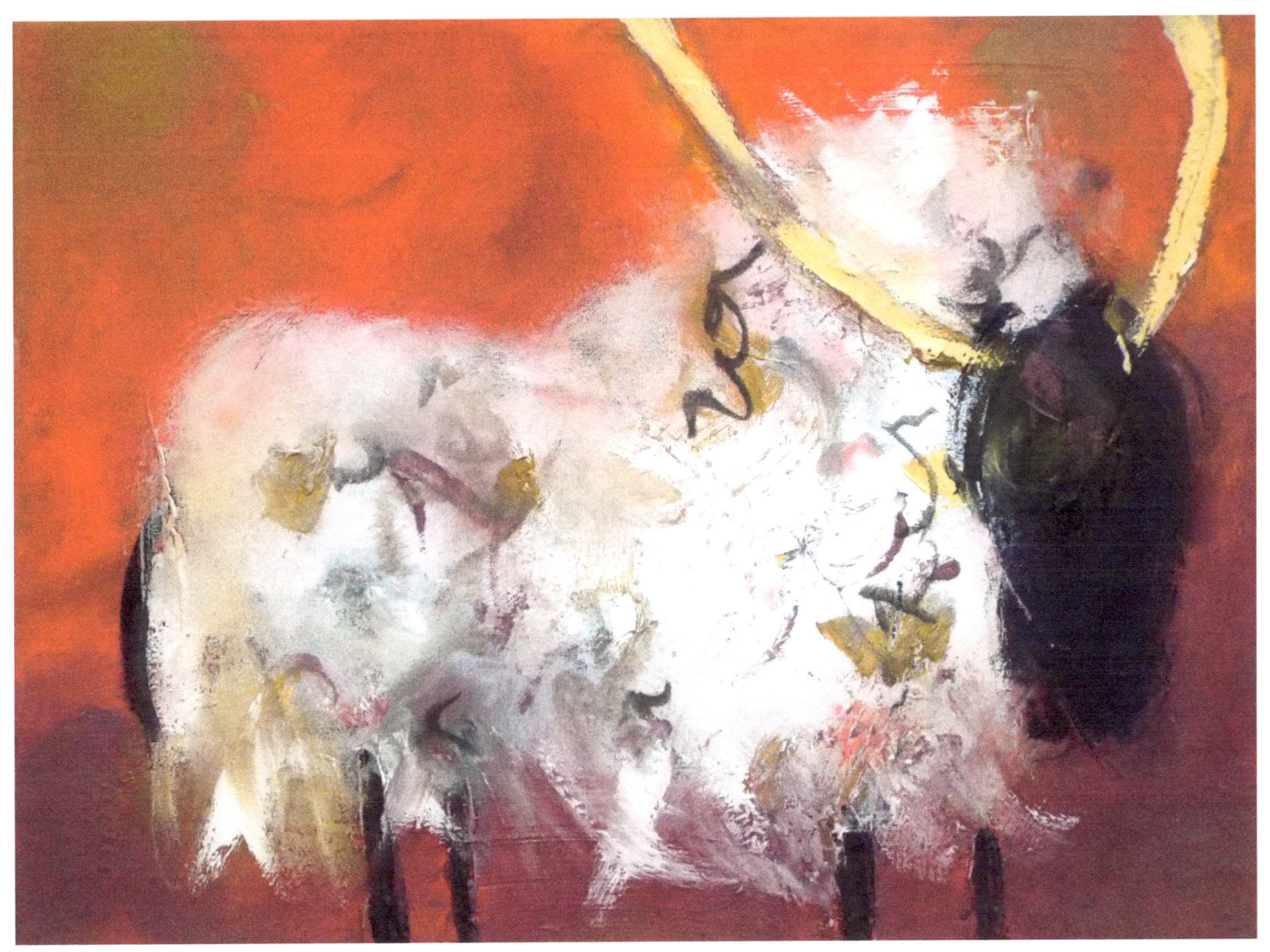

Spotted Goat, 2020
Oil on canvas, 16 x 20 inches

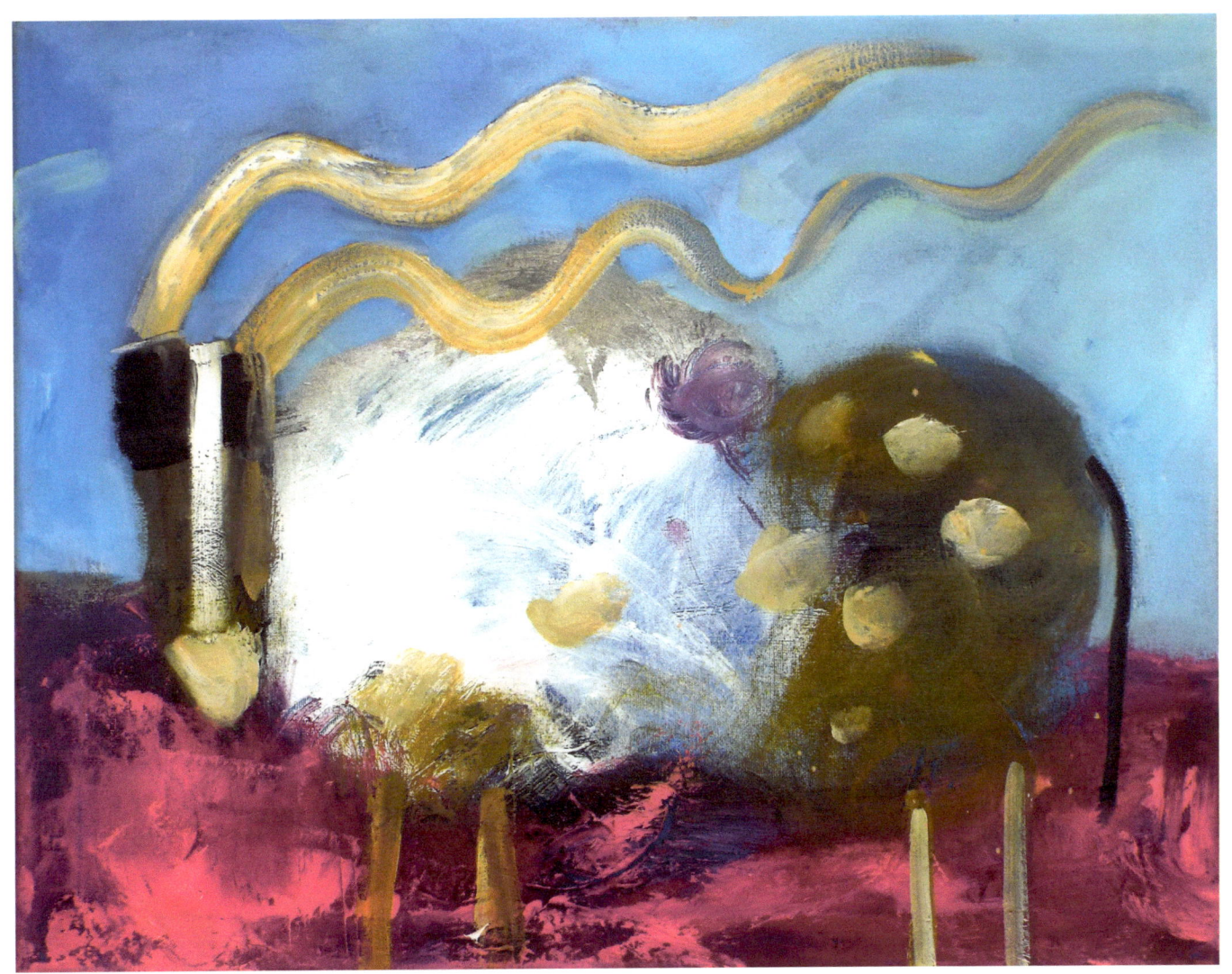

Spiral Horned Goat, 2020
Oil on paper, 22 x 30 inches

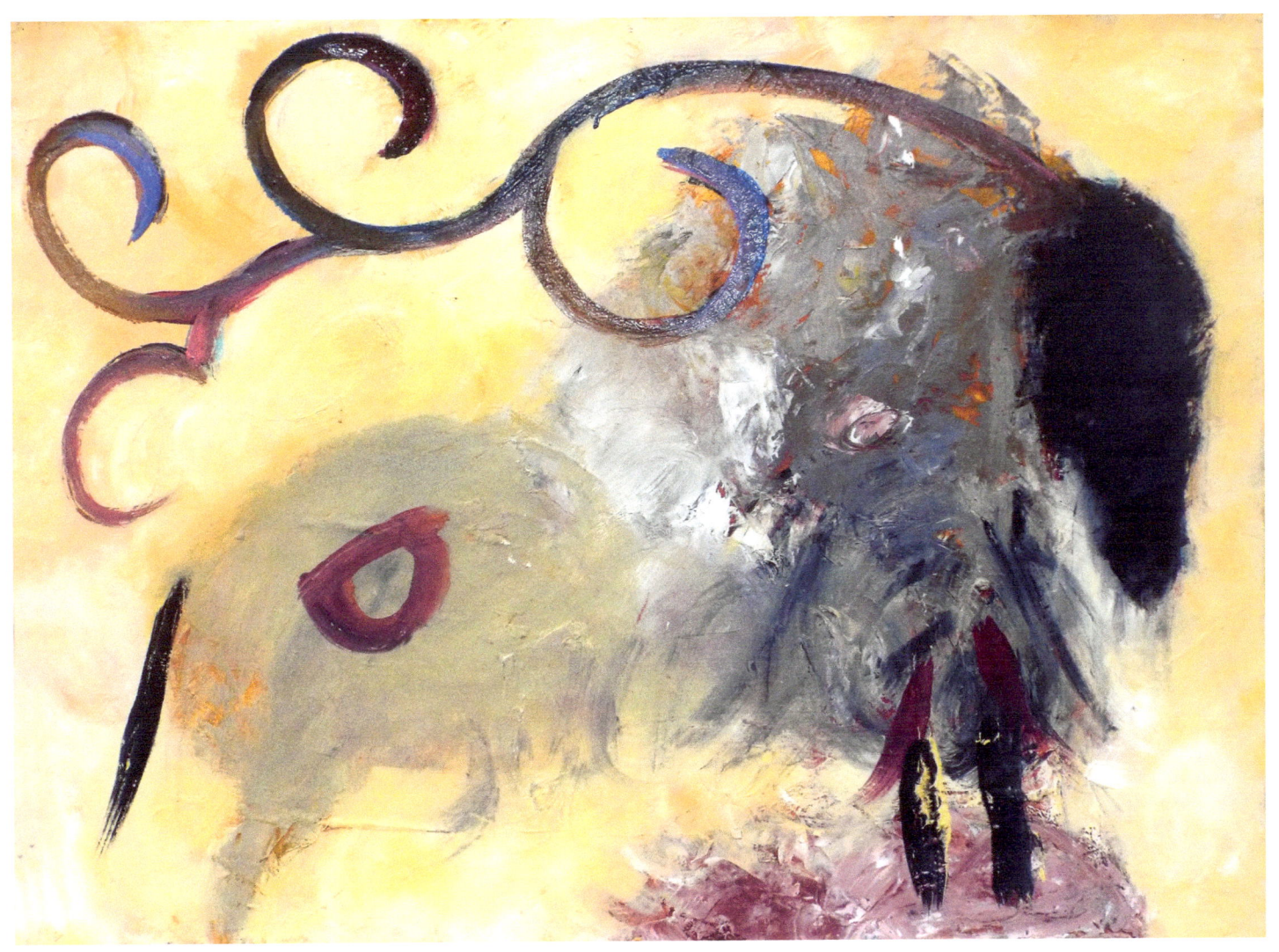

Tricolor Bison, 2020
Oil on paper, 14.75 x 20 inches

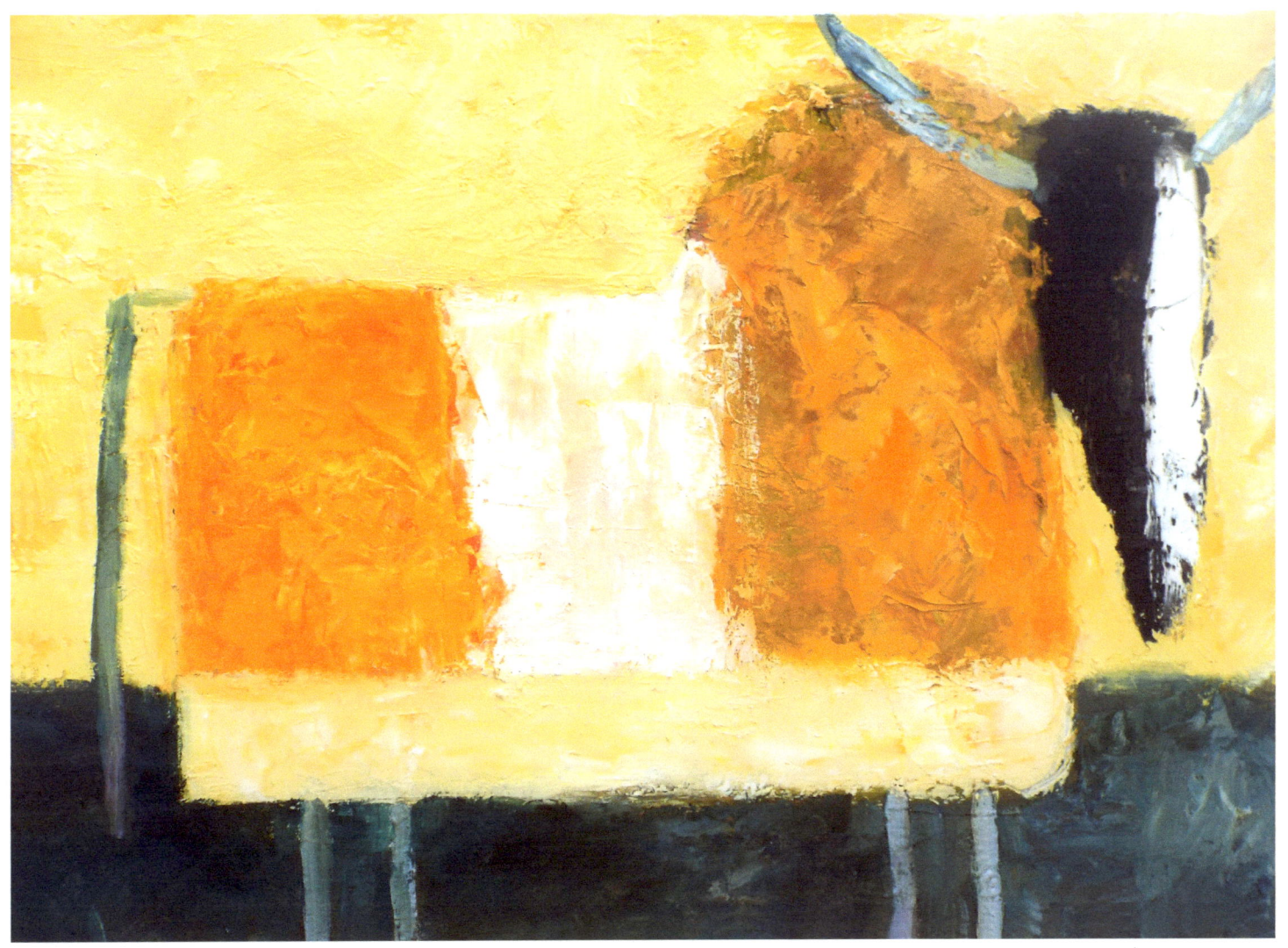

Turning Stag with Rose Antlers, 2020
Oil on paper, 22 x 30 inches

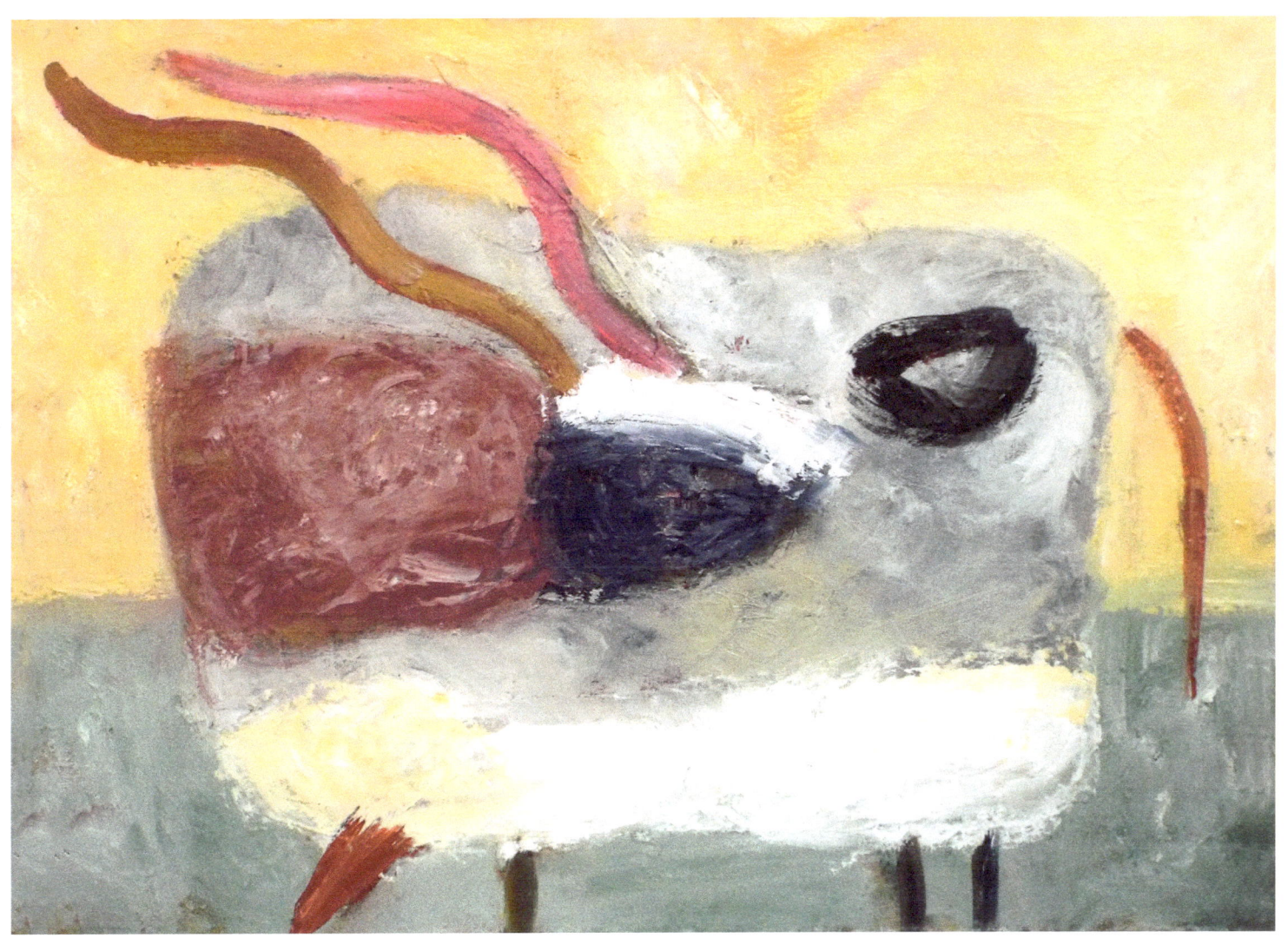

Red and White Antlred Stag, 2020
Oil on canvas, 12 x 16 inches

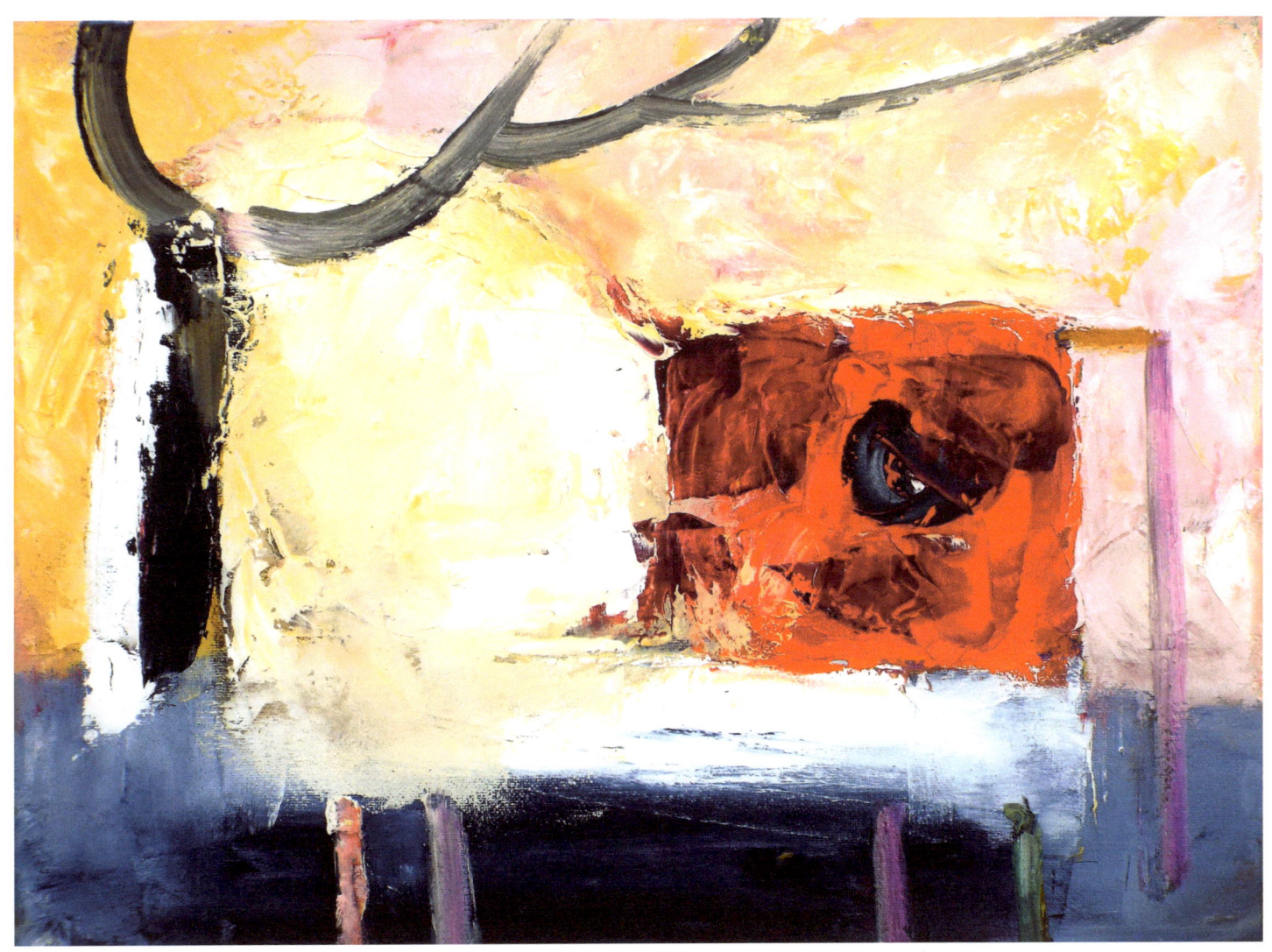

Addax in Blue Field, 2019
Oil on canvas, 14 x 11 inches

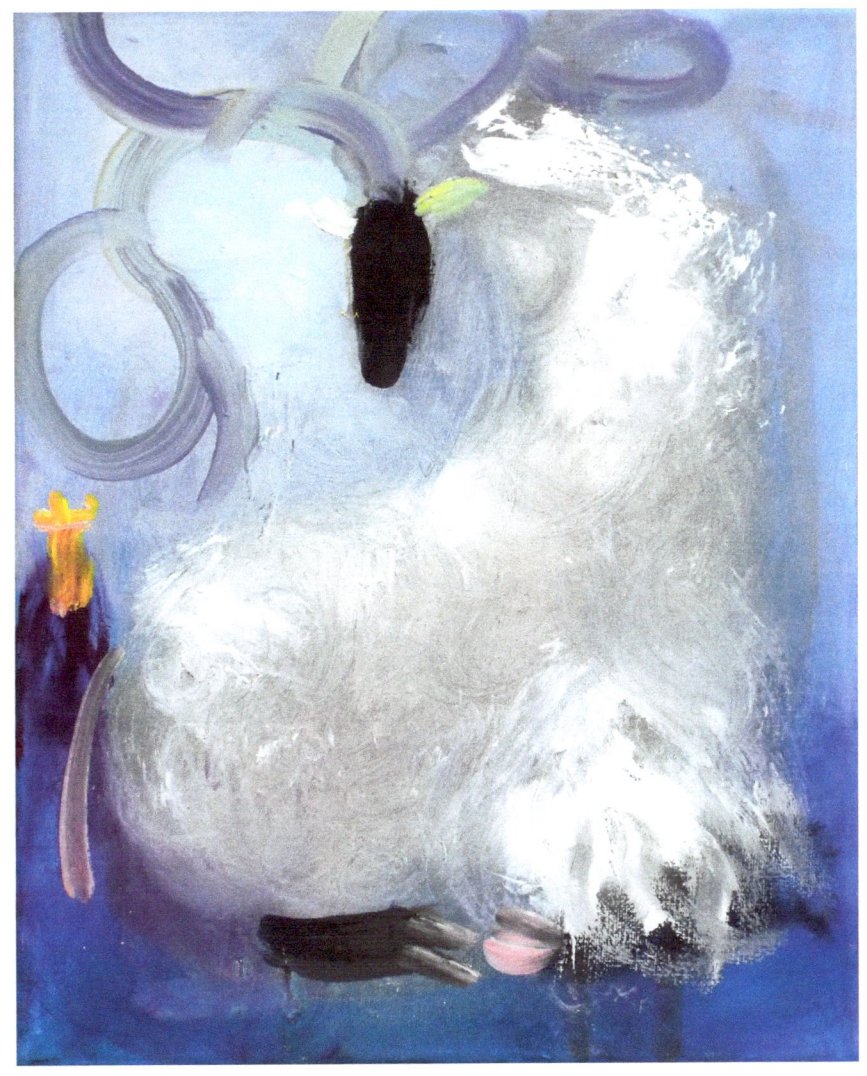

Blue Marsh Deer with Branching Antlers, 2019
Oil on canvas, 14 x 11 inches

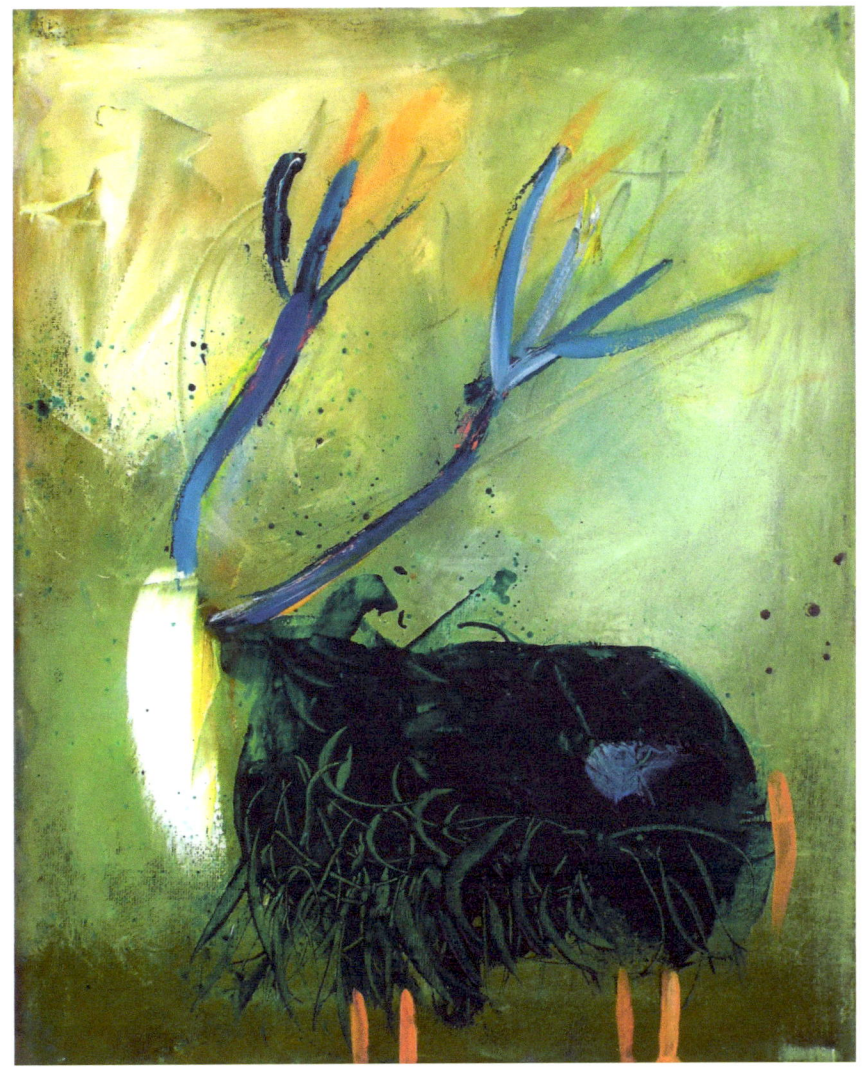

Rose Antlered Forest Deer, 2019
Oil on canvas, 14 x 11 inches

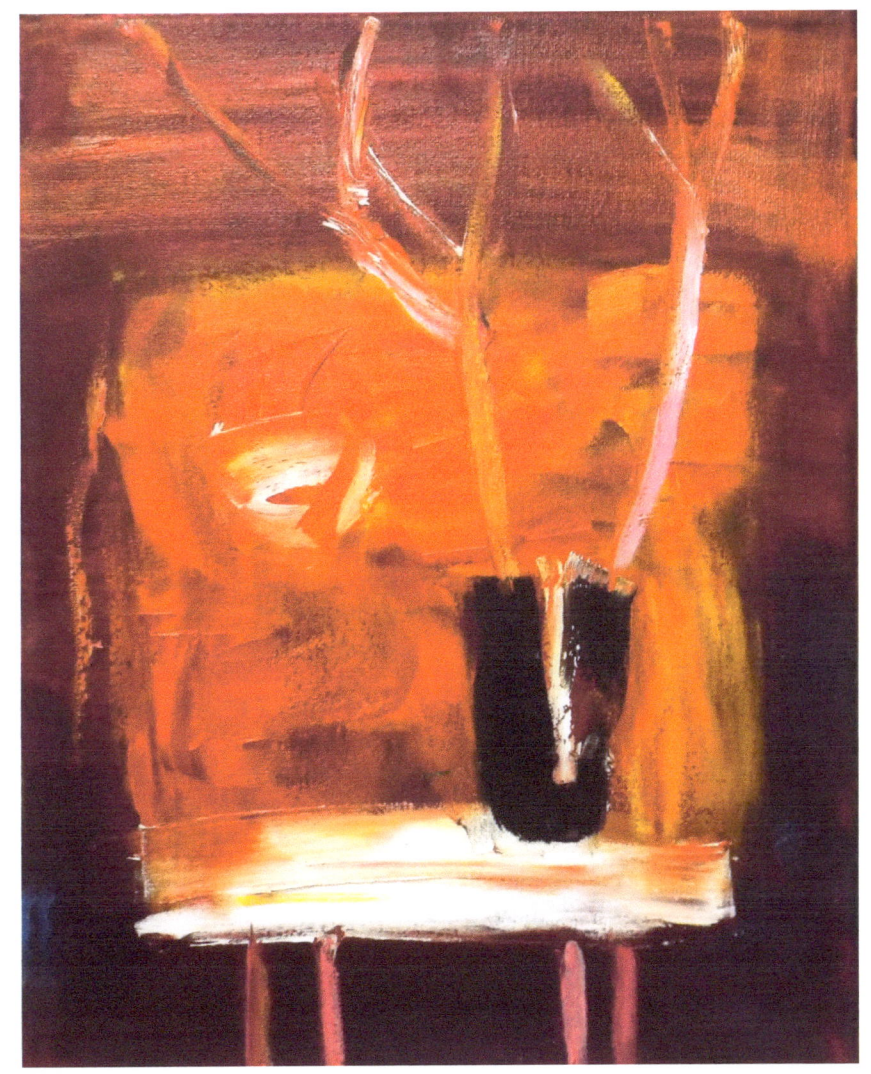

White Spotted Bison, 2020
Oil on canvas, 14 x 11 inches

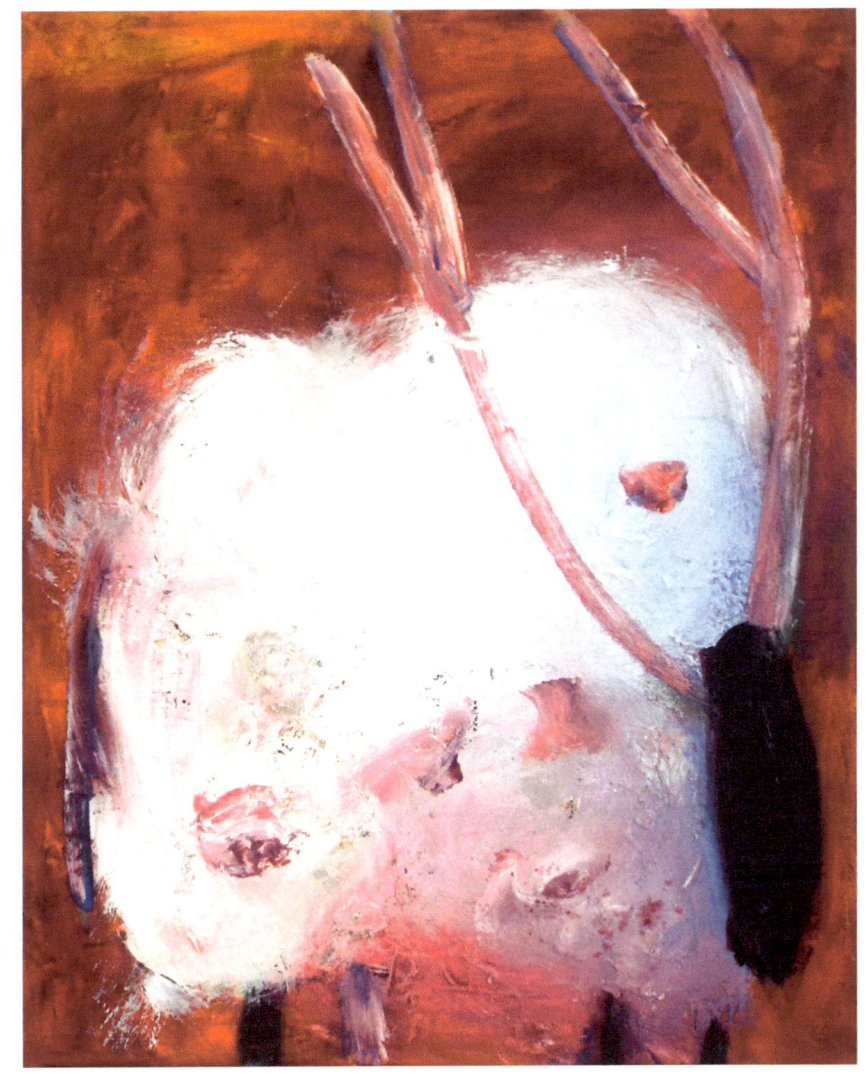

Lyre Horned Bison, 2020
Oil on canvas, 12 x 16 inches

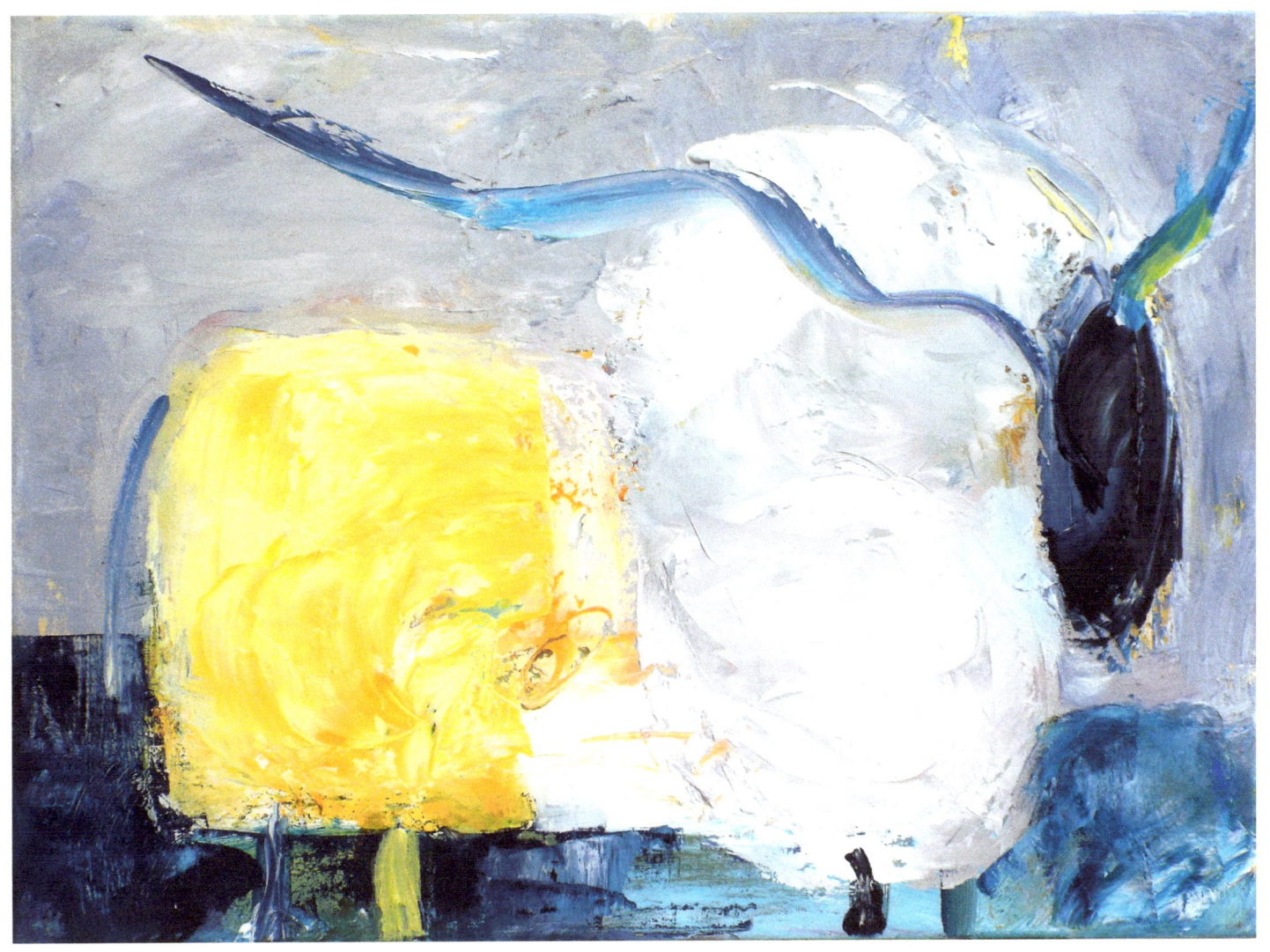

Athenian Goat, 2018
Oil on canvas, 22 x 30 inches

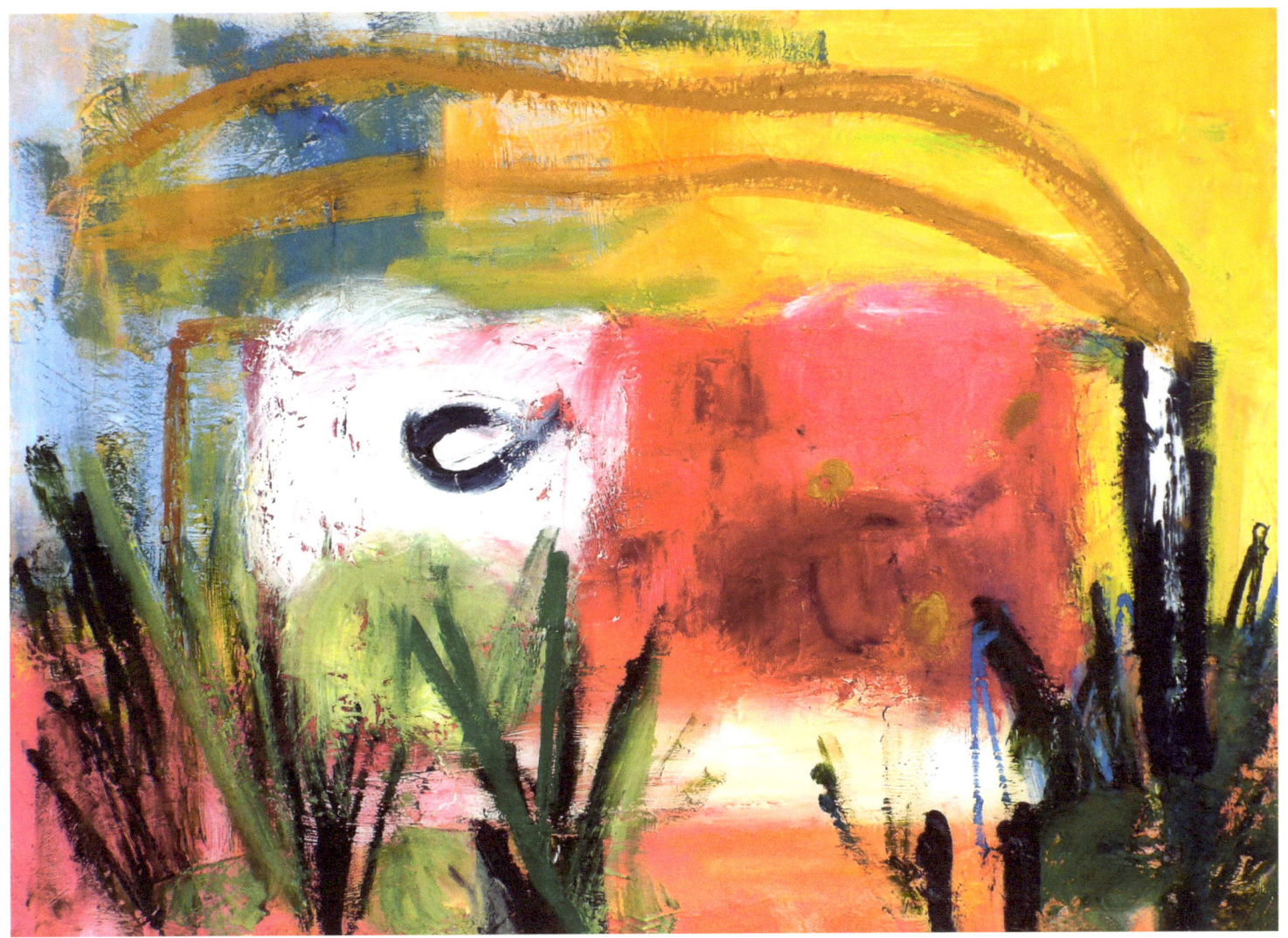

Blue Antlered Temple Deer, 2020
Oil on paper, 22 x 30 inches

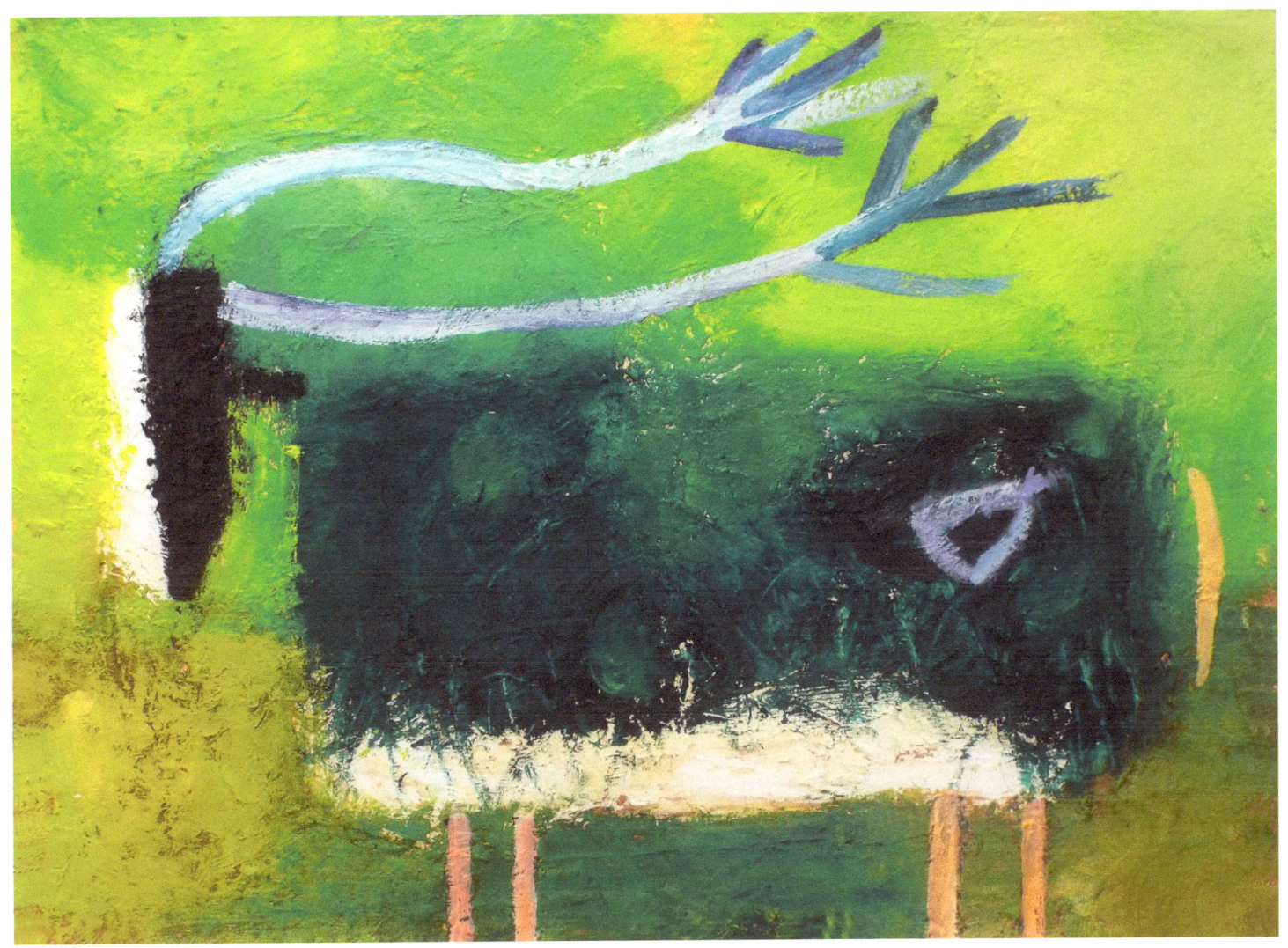

Gray Spotted Antelope in Magenta Field, 2020
Oil on canvas, 12 x 16 inches

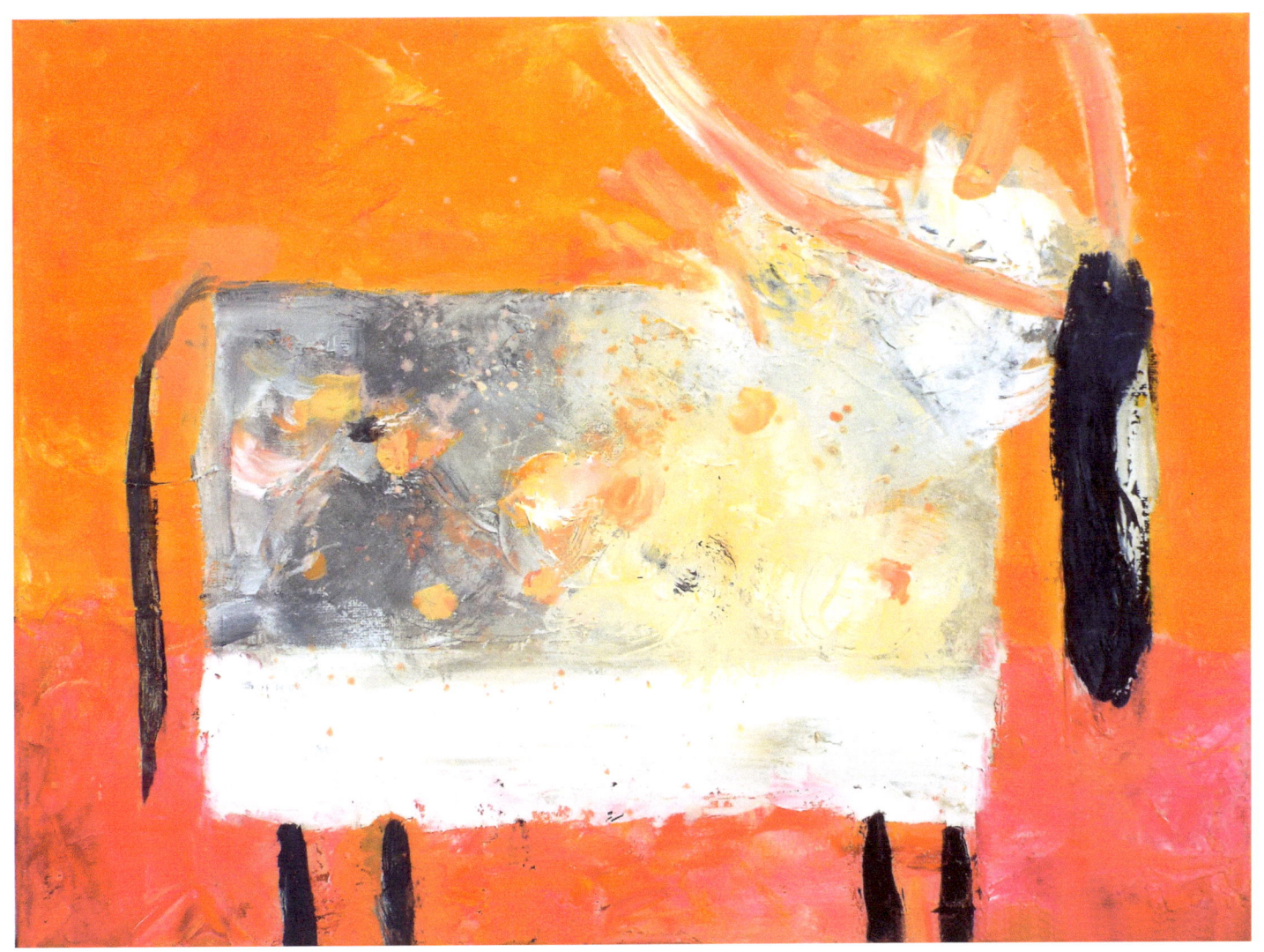

Goat with Fluted Horns, 2019
Oil on canvas, 14 x 11 inches

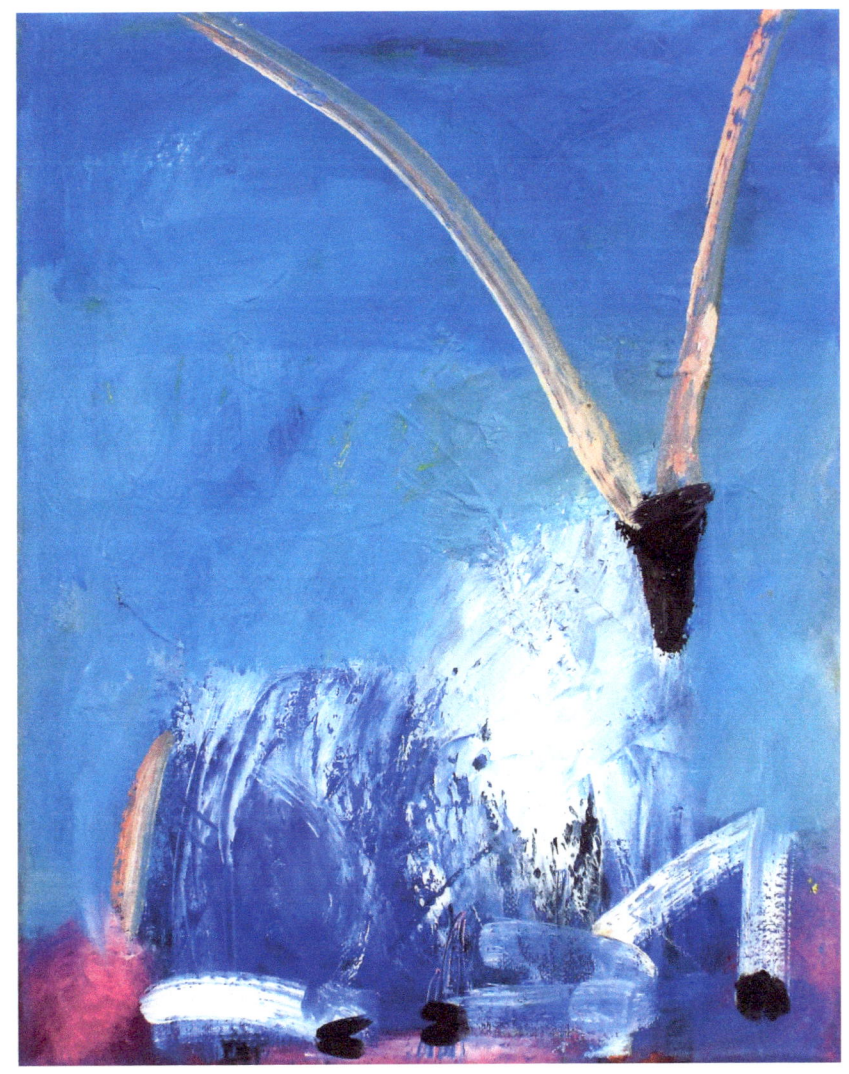

White Speckled Antelope in Magenta Field, 2020
Oil on canvas, 14 x 11 inches

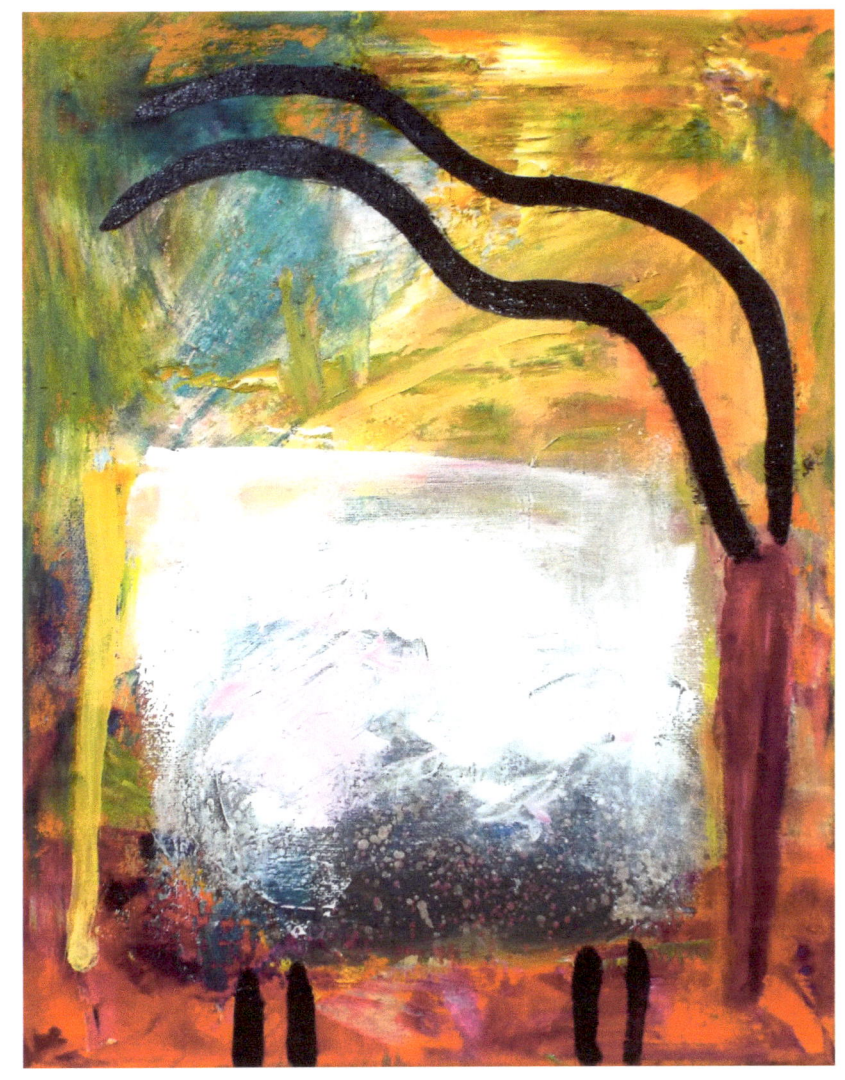

Red Antlered Stag, 2020
Oil on canvas, 11 x 14 inches

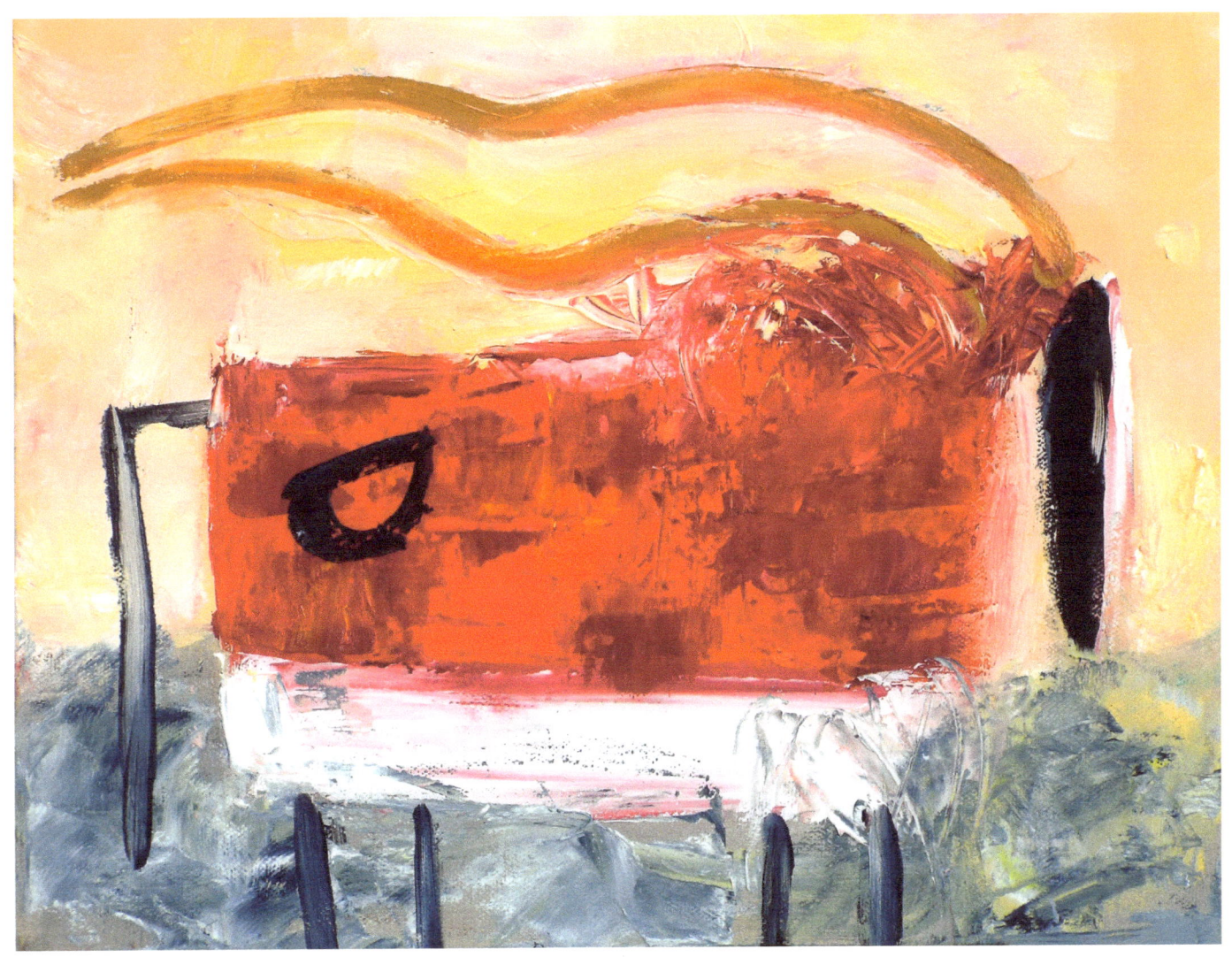

Split Stag in Red Field, 2018
Oil on canvas, 30 x 22 inches

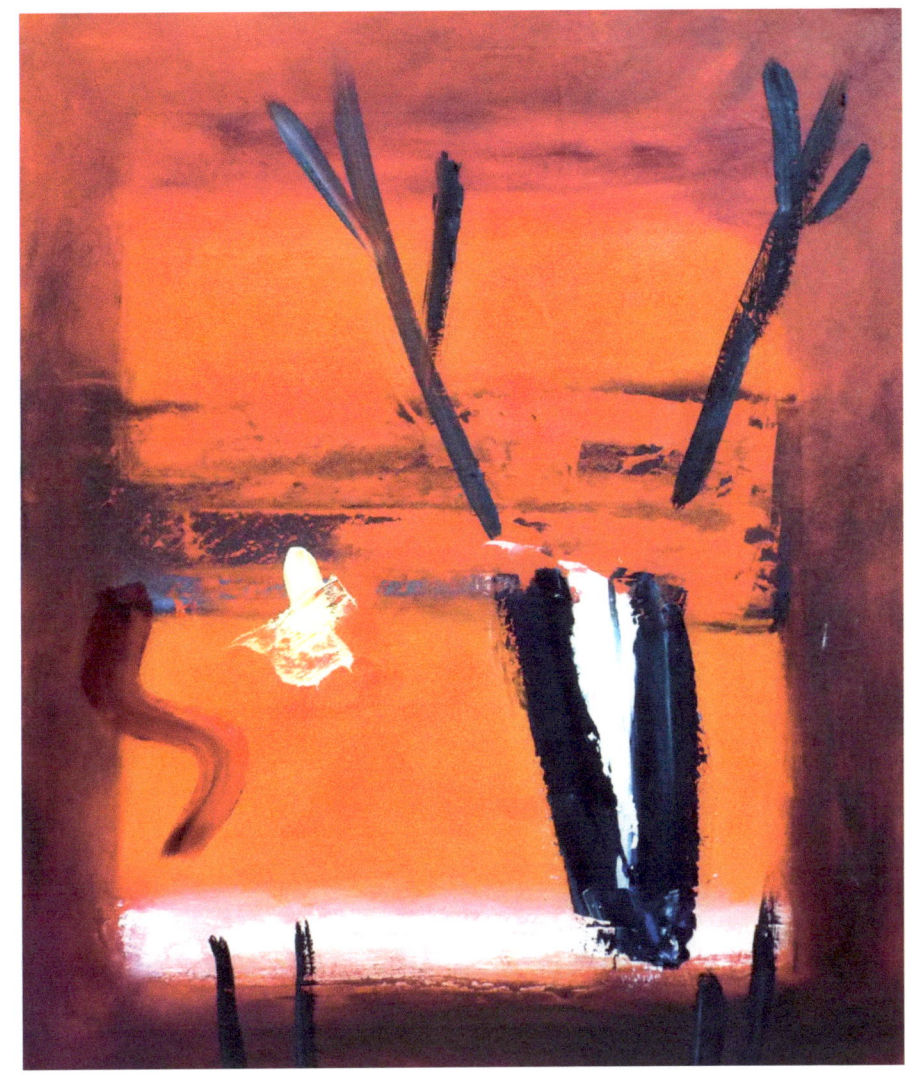

Monotypes

Red Goat in Ochre Field, 2014
Monotype, 10 x 8 inches

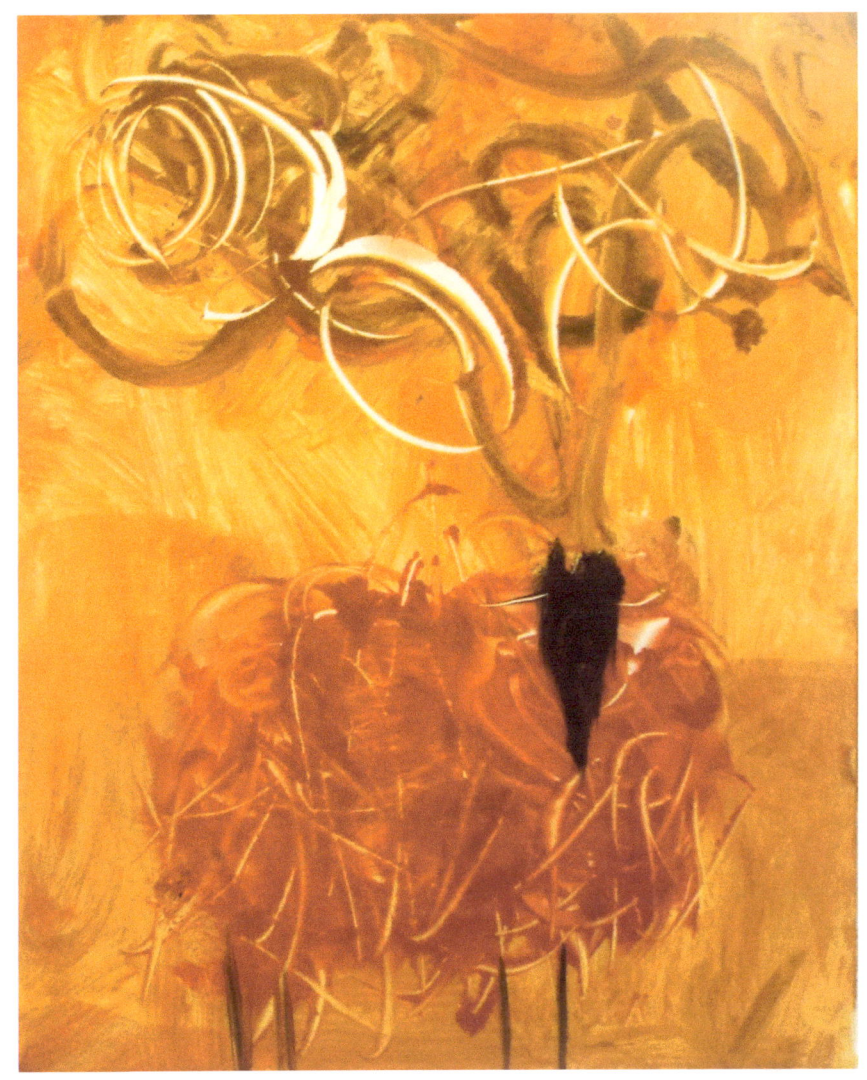

Tien Shan Goat, 2014
Monotype, 10 x 8 inches

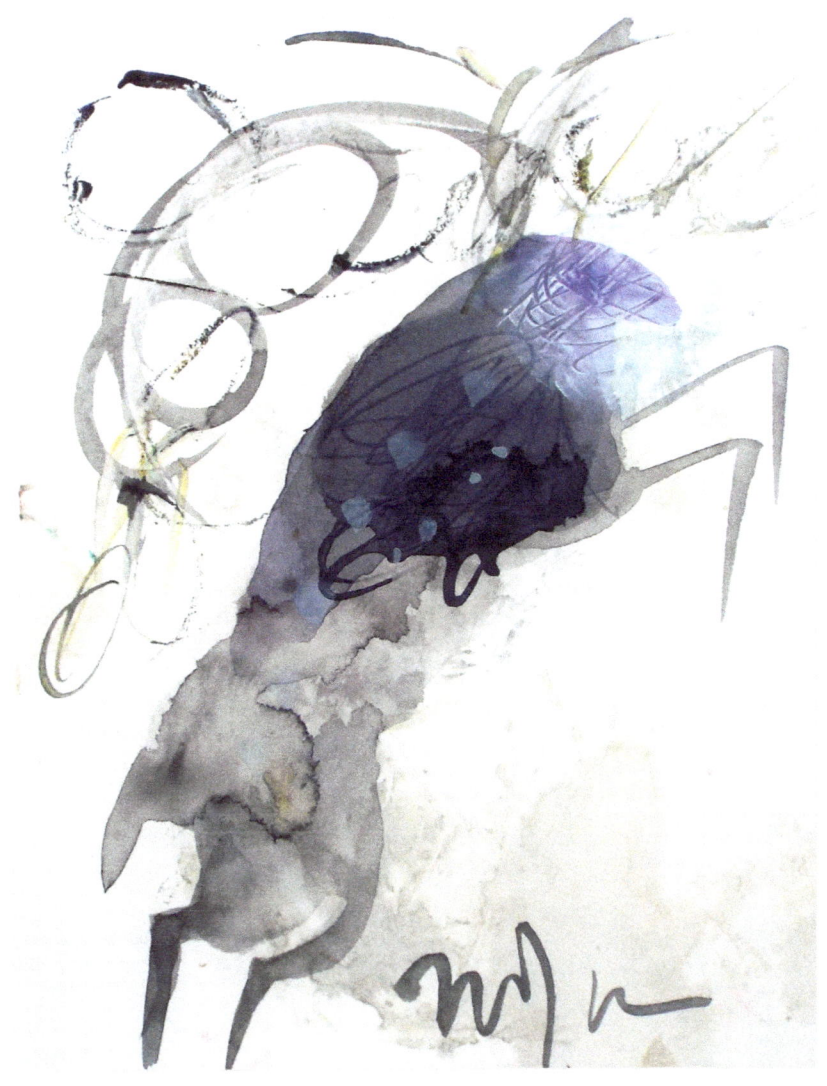

Himalayan Goat, 2018
Monotype and chine-collé, 8 x 10 inches

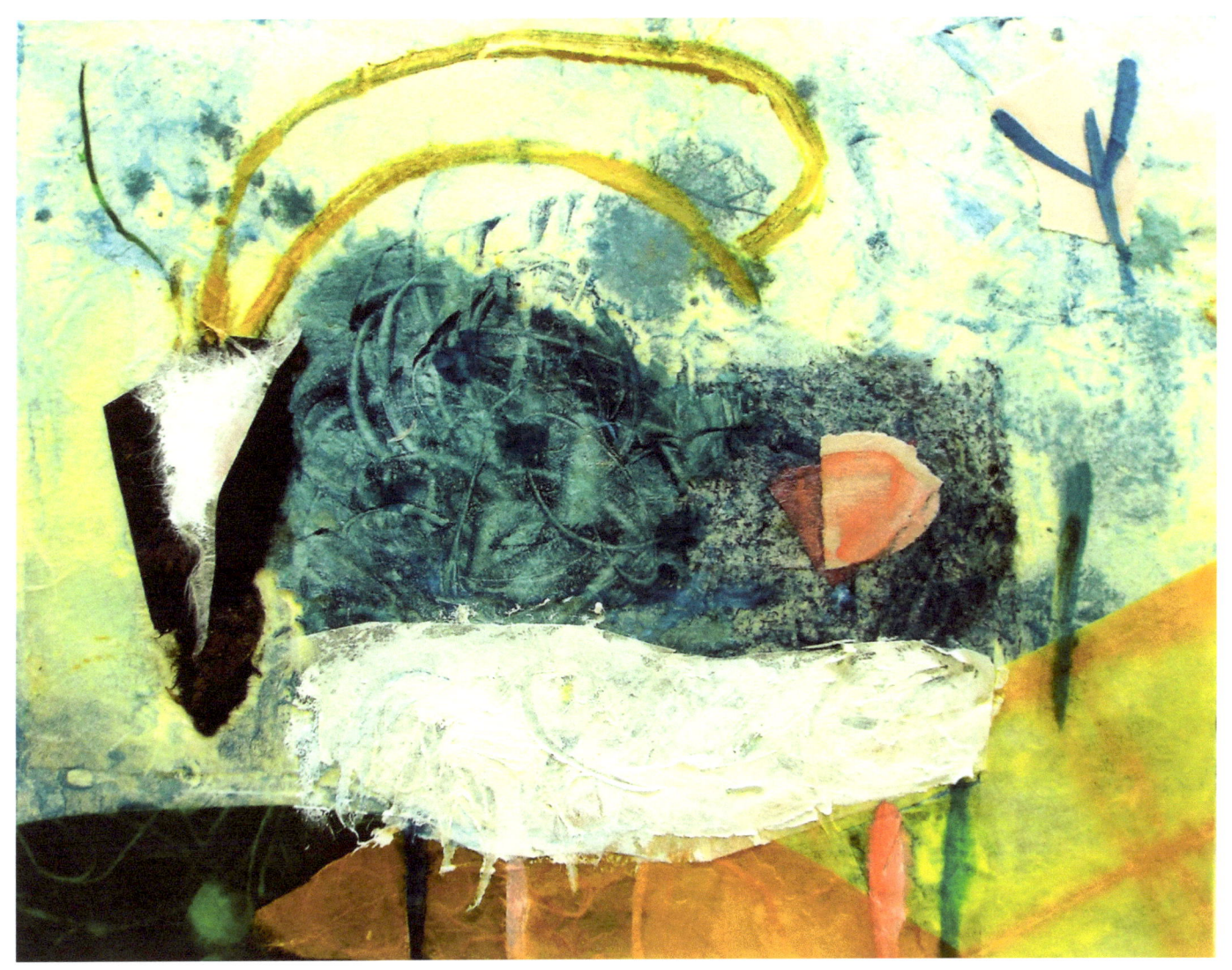

Blue Stag, 2014
Monotype, 10 x 8 inches

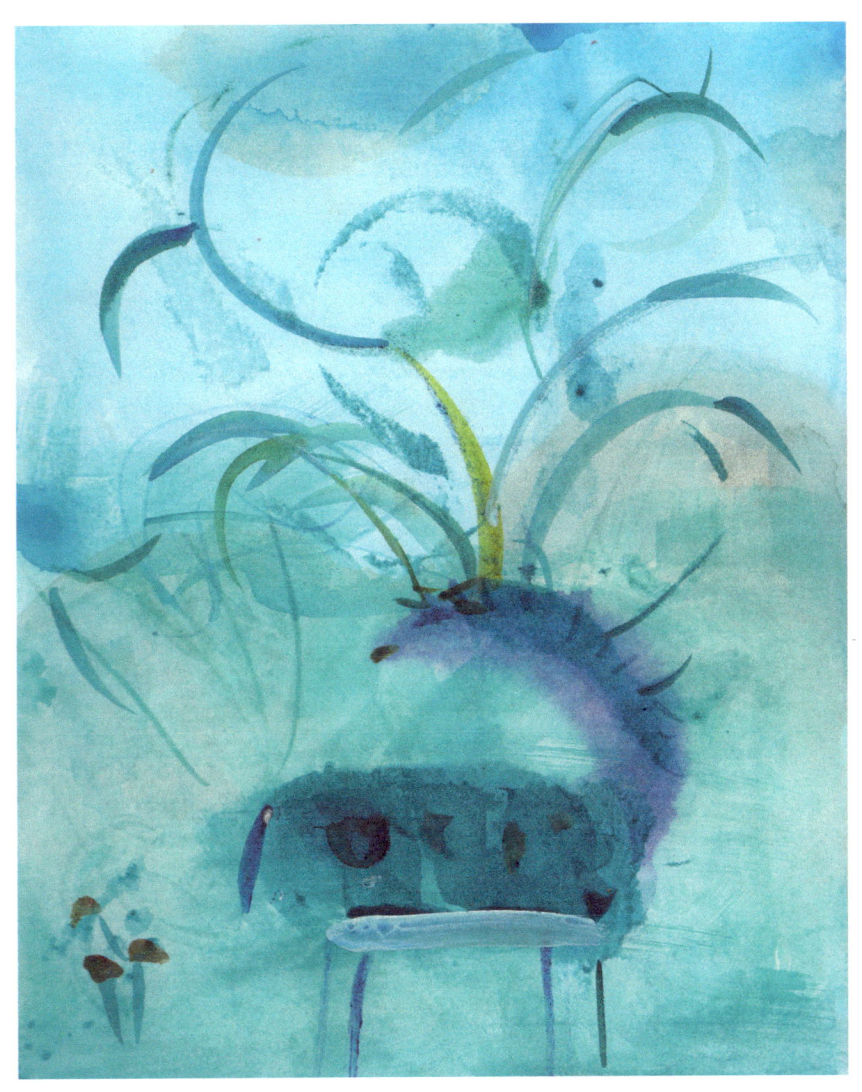

EDUCATION

1974 Goddard College, New York City, B.A; M.A. 1977

ONE-PERSON EXHIBITIONS (unless otherwise noted)

2020 "Horned & Antlered Animals", Abingdon Square Viewing Room,
   online exhibition, New York, NY
2016 "Journeys", Carter Burden Gallery, New York, NY (two-person show)
2008 "Mongolian Horses & Siberian Tigers", Cheryl Pelavin Fine Arts, New York, NY
   "Cambodian Flower Archaeology Monotypes", Cheryl Pelavin Fine Arts, New York, NY
2007 "The Cambodian Journal", Java Cafe Gallery, Phnom Penh, Cambodia
2006 "Review: Cranes, Herons and Waterbirds", Cheryl Pelavin Fine Arts, New York, NY
   "Preview: Rainforests, Cloudforests and Pine", Cheryl Pelavin Fine Arts, New York, NY
   "Paintings", College of the Marshall Islands, Majuro, Republic of the Marshall Islands
2005 "The Crane Series", Ogilvie-Pertl Gallery, Chicago, IL
   "Riverbirds & Rainforests", The National Academies of Sciences Gallery,
     Washington, DC
   "Materia Medica", The Creative Center, New York, NY
2004 "The Crane & Heron Series", Cheryl Pelavin Fine Arts, New York, NY
   "Paintings by Valentina DuBasky", Friesen Fine Arts, Sun Valley, ID
   "Atlantic Flyway Project", Teaneck Creek Conservancy, Teaneck, NJ
2002 "New Paintings", Hodges Taylor Gallery, Charlotte, NC
   "New Paintings", Friesen Fine Arts, Sun Valley, ID
2001 "New Paintings", Silpakorn University Art Center Gallery, Bangkok, Thailand
   "Orchids & Fossils: New Landscape Paintings", Cheryl Pelavin Fine Arts, New York, NY
2000 "Ancient Futures: New Paintings & Monoprints", Cheryl Pelavin Fine Arts, New York, NY
   "Representation Debut," Friesen Fine Arts, Seattle, WA
   "Orchids on the Way to the Temple", Galerie Timothy Tew, Atlanta, GA
   "Through Bending Trees", Friesen Fine Arts, Sun Valley, ID
1998 "Memory & Light: New Paintings", Cheryl Pelavin Fine Arts, New York, NY
   "Materia Medica: New Monoprints", Cheryl Pelavin Fine Arts, New York, NY
1997 "Paintings", Hodges Taylor Gallery, Charlotte, NC
   "Landscape, Archaeology & Memory, Paintings, Sculpture & Monoprints 1985-97",
     University of North Carolina Gallery, Asheville, NC
1995 "Painting Retrospective", Rena Haveson Gallery, Pittsburgh, PA
   "Photographs", Gallery f32, Asheville, NC
1991 "New Paintings", Ruth Siegel Gallery, New York, NY
1990 "New Paintings", Ruth Siegel Gallery, New York, NY
1987 "Bronze Sculpture from the Caravan Series", Empire Bronze Art Gallery, LIC, NY
1986 "Paintings on Paper", Oscarsson-Siegeltuch Gallery, New York, NY
   "Paintings & Monotypes", Hodges Banks Gallery, Seattle, WA
1985 "Recent Paintings", van Straaten Gallery, Chicago, IL
   "Recent Paintings", Oscarsson Hood Gallery, New York, NY
   "Paintings from the Stag Series", Gloria Luria Gallery, Miami, FL
   "Monotypes", Jay Gallery, New York, NY
1984 "Recent Paintings", Susan Montazenos Gallery, Philadelphia, PA
1983 "Paintings from the Stag Series", Oscarsson Hood Gallery, New York, NY
   "Recent Paintings", Robert L. Kidd Gallery, Detroit, MI
1981 "Paintings on Paper", Oscarsson Hood Gallery, New York, NY
1980 "Paintings", Semaphore Gallery, New York, NY

GROUP EXHIBITIONS

2020 "Monoprint 2020 - Printers and Presses", Washington Art Association & Gallery,
     Washington Depot, CT
2019 "The Black and White Show", 11 Jane St. Art Center, Saugerties, NY
2018 "United States Embassy Exhibition", Art in Embassies Program,
     United States Embassy, Beijing, China
   "Collective Memory", Equity Gallery, New York, NY
2017 "The Trace", Lichtundfire Gallery, New York, NY
   "Westbeth Winter Exhibition" Westbeth Gallery, New York, NY
2015 "True Monotypes", International Print Center of New York, curated by
     Janice Oresman, New York, NY
   "Small Works", Carter Burden Gallery, New York, NY
   "Group Exhibition", McElwain Fine Arts, St Louis, MO
2014 "Shifting Ecologies", The Painting Center, New York, NY
   "Tandem Press Monoprints", Expo Chicago, IL
   "Tandem Press Monoprints", IFPDA Print Fair, New York Armory, New York, NY
   "Tandem Press Monoprints", NYINK Art Fair, Miami Beach, FL
2013 "Tandem Press Monoprints", IFPDA Print Fair, New York Armory, New York, NY
   "Tandem Press Monoprints", NYINK Art Fair, Miami Beach, FL
2010 "Spring Prints", Cheryl Pelavin Fine Arts, New York, NY
2009 "Paintings", Friesen Fine Arts, Seattle, WA
   "Streetscapes", Landscapes, Still Lives, Jan Larsen Art, New York, NY
   "Art and Democracy", Gallery H, New York, NY

2008	"Friends", Cheryl Pelavin Fine Arts, New York, NY	2000	"Group Exhibition", Friesen Fine Art, Sun Valley, ID
	"From Different Horizons of Rock Shelter", Pang Mapha Archaeological Site, Pang Mapha, Thailand	1999	"United States Embassy Exhibition", Art in Embassies Program, United States Embassy, Lima, Peru
	"From Different Horizons of Rock Shelter", National Gallery of Art, Bangkok, Thailand		"United States Embassy Exhibition", Art in Embassies Program, United States Embassy, Reykjavik, Iceland
	"Print Show", Cheryl Pelavin Fine Arts, New York, NY		"United States Embassy Exhibition", Art in Embassies Program, United States, Embassy, Bangkok, Thailand
2007	"25 Years of Printmaking at Cheryl Pelavin Fine Arts", Cheryl Pelavin Fine Arts, NY, NY		"Sitting Pretty", Met Life Windows, New York, NY
2006	"Alignment", Friesen Fine Art, Seattle, WA		"Birdsong", Laurie Seeman Gallery, Nyack, NY
	"Oil & Wax", Robert Roman Galleries, Scottsdale, AZ	1998	"Visual Dialogues: 15 Women Artists", Robert Kidd Gallery, Detroit, MI
	"Group Show", Ogilvie-Pertl Gallery, Chicago, IL		"Nature/Culture", The New York Arts Exchange Show, New York, NY
	"Art Scottsdale", Ogilvie-Pertl Gallery & Larsen Gallery, Scottsdale, AZ		"Four Artists", Lone Star Park Gallery, Dallas, TX
	"Traveling Exhibition: Agent Orange: Consequence of War, a Call to Conscience", Marlboro College Gallery, Vermont; Brandeis University Gallery, Boston; George Washington University Gallery, Washington, DC		"Group Exhibition", Tower Air, curated by Jeannie Greenberg, New York, NY
2005	"Oil & Wax: Chapter & Verse", Siano Gallery, Philadelphia, PA	1997	"Sizzle", Jeffrey Coploff Gallery, New York, NY
2004	"Two Artists", Ogilvie-Pertl Gallery, Chicago, IL		"Group Exhibition", Hillwood Museum, Chattanooga, TN
	"The New Realism", Robert L. Kidd Gallery, Detroit, MI		"Art of Hearts", Nora Haime Gallery & the National Academy of Design, New York, NY
	"Two Artists: Reflections of Cambodia", The Puffin Foundation, Teaneck, NJ		"Group Exhibition", Hodges Taylor Gallery, Charlotte, NC
	"Returning the Brownfields of Teaneck Creek", Teaneck Creek Conservancy, Teaneck, NJ		"The National Horse Show", Robert Kidd Gallery, Detroit, MI
	"Toxic Landscape", Long Beach Island Foundation of Arts & Sciences, Love Ladies, NJ	1996	"Partners in Printmaking: Works from Solo Impressions", National Museum of Women in the Arts, Washington, DC
	"Lower Manhattan Cultural Council Benefit", DK, New York, New York, NY		"Painting Exhibition", Hillwood Museum, Long Island University, NY
	"Dealer's Choice", Robert L. Kidd Gallery, Detroit, MI		"Three Photographers", June Kelly Gallery, New York, NY
2003	"Flora and Fauna: Manifestations", Cheryl Pelavin Fine Arts, New York, NY		"United States Embassy Exhibition", Art in Embassies Program, United States Embassy, Muscat, Oman
	"United States Embassy Exhibition", Art in Embassies Program, United States Embassy, Panama City, Panama		"Recent Monotype Editions", Pelavin Editions, New York, NY
2002	"United States Embassy Exhibition", Art in Embassies Program, United States Embassy Riga, Latvia		"Group Exhibition", Robert L. Kidd Gallery, Detroit, MI
	"United States Embassy Exhibition", Art in Embassies Program, United States Embassy, Tallinn, Estonia	1995	"United States Embassy Exhibition", Art in Embassies Program, United States Embassy, Amman, Jordan
	"Two Artists", Friesen Fine Art, Seattle, WA		"Inaugural Exhibition", Michele Bigue Gallery, Fort Lauderdale, FL
	"Fifteenth Anniversary Exhibition", Galerie Timothy Tew, Atlanta, GE	1994	"United States Embassy Exhibition", Art in Embassies Program, United States Embassy, Oslo, Norway
	"Affordable Art Fair", Cheryl Pelavin Fine Arts, New York, NY		"Group Exhibition", ES Painting Space, New York, NY
	"The Head Show", Galerie Timothy Tew, Atlanta, GE	1993	"Animal Imagery", Champion Paper, curated by Janice Oresman, Hartfield, CT
	"Reactions", Exit Art, New York, NY	1992	"34 Raumes", Documenta, Berlin, Germany
	"Toxic Landscape: Artists Look at the Environment", Bibliotéca Nacional José Martí, Havana, Cuba		"Printmaking from the Permanent Collection", Jane Voorhees Zimmerli Art Museum, Rutgers University, NJ
2001	"World Trade Center Benefit Exhibition", Cheryl Pelavin Fine Arts, New York, NY		"Works on Paper from Pelavin Editions", The Armory Show, New York, NY
	"Group Exhibition", Friesen Fine Art, Seattle, WA	1991	"Works on Paper", Champion Paper, Stanford, CT
	"Group Exhibition", Norton Gallery, Seattle, WA		

1990 "Intaglio Printing in the 1980's", Jane Voorhees Zimmerli Art Museum, Rutgers University, New Brunswick, NJ
"Women in Print", Traveling museum exhibition, National Museum of Women in the Arts, Washington, DC
"Menagerie", General Electric Company Headquarters, curated by MOMA Advisory Services, CT
1989 "Surface Printing in the 1980's", Jane Voorhees Zimmerli Art Museum, Rutgers University, New Brunswick, NJ
"Creatures", Benson Gallery, Bridgehampton, NY
1988 "Three Sculptors Working in Bronze", Gallerie Helene Grubair, Miami, FL
1987 "Group Show", Albright Knox Museum, Buffalo, NY
1986 "Monotypes by Gallery Artists", Oscarsson-Siegeltuch Gallery, New York, NY
"Paintings", van Straaten Gallery, Chicago, IL
"Inaugural Exhibition", Group Show, Oscarsson-Siegeltuch Gallery, New York, NY
"Homage to Ana Mendieta", Zeus Trabia Gallery, New York, NY
"Monotypes", Jay Gallery, New York, NY
1985 "Art of the 70's & 80's", Aldrich Museum of Contemporary Art, Ridgefield, CT
"1985 Invitational Quinquennial Exhibition", Oscarsson Hood Gallery, New York, NY
"Selections from the Jane Voorhees Zimmerli Art Museum", The Grolier Club, NY, NY
"Chicago Art Expo", Oscarsson Hood Gallery, Chicago, IL
"Pelavin Editions 1985", Jay Gallery, New York, NY
"Monotypes & Works on Paper", Robert L. Kidd Gallery, Detroit, MI
"Animals: Contemporary Visions", Robert L. Kidd Gallery, Detroit, MI
"The Animal Within", Jay Gallery, New York, NY
"Young Printmakers", Roger Ramsey Gallery, Chicago, IL
"Two Artists", Peri Renneth Gallery, West Hampton, NY
1984 "Painting Invitational", Robeson Center Gallery, Rutgers University, New Brunswick, NJ
"Situations", Jamaica Arts Center, The Newark Museum Collection, New York, NY
"Review/Preview", Oscarsson Hood Gallery, New York, NY
"Works on Paper", Wolff Gallery, New York, NY
"8 at 84", Robert Feldman Gallery, New York, NY
"Works on Paper", Barbara Greene Gallery, Miami, FL
"Ringing in the New", Jay Gallery, New York, NY
1983 "New Acquisitions", Newark Museum, Newark, NJ
"Art on Paper", Weatherspoon Museum, Greensboro, NC
"Group Exhibition", Oscarsson Hood Gallery, New York, NY
"Works on Paper", Frumpkin Struve Gallery, Chicago, IL
"Group Show", Albright Knox Museum, Buffalo, NY
1982 "Group Show", Albright Knox Museum, Buffalo, NY
"New Acquisitions", Alternative Museum, New York, NY
"Mixed Bag", Alternative Museum, New York, NY
"Group Exhibition", McNay Art Institute, Collectors Gallery VI, Austin, TX
"Works on Paper", Roger Ramsey Gallery, Chicago, IL
"Group Exhibition", Oscarsson Hood Gallery, New York, NY
1981 "New Acquisitions", Aldrich Museum of Contemporary Art, CT
"Nine Artists Invited", Meisal Gallery, New York, NY
"Group Exhibition", Semaphore Gallery, New York, NY
"The Working Process", O.I.A. Exhibition, New York, NY
"Group Exhibition", Newcomber Westreich Gallery, Washington, DC
1980 "Small Works", 80 Gallery, Washington Square East, New York, NY
"Group Show," Race Gallery, Philadelphia, PA
"4 Artists", Soho Center for Visual Artists, New York, NY
"Betty Parsons at Robert L. Kidd Gallery", Robert L. Kidd Gallery, Detroit, MI

MUSEUM COLLECTIONS

Alternative Museum, New York, NY
Herbert F. Johnson Museum, Cornell University, Ithaca, NY
National Museum of Women in the Arts, Washington, DC
Newark Museum, Newark, NJ
Orlando Museum of Art, Orlando, FL
Seattle Art Museum, Seattle, WA
Jane Voorhees Zimmerli Art Museum, Rutgers, NJ
Xianghai Museum, Xianghai Nature Reserve, Xianghai, China

SELECTED PUBLIC COLLECTIONS

Agrace Hospice Care, Madison, WI
Architectural Arts, Inc, Dallas, TX
Banca della Suizzeria Italiana, New York, NY
Bank Boston, Boston, MA
Barron & Budd, New York, NY
Chase Manhattan Bank, New York, NY
Chemical Bank, New York, NY
Citibank International, Miami, FL

Denrich Leasing Company, Miami, FL
Echo Lab, MN
Carey Ellis Company, MN
Ernst & Young, New York, NY
Evergreen Asset & Management Corporation, New York, NY
Federal Reserve Bank, Chicago, IL
First National Bank, Boston, MA
Fuzhou International Center, Fuzhou, China
General Instruments, New York, NY
General Mills, Inc, Minneapolis, MN
Goldman-Sachs, New York, NY
Gruntal, New York, NY
Henson & Effron, St. Paul, MN
Hospital Corporation of North America, Nashville, TN
IBM Collection, Los Angeles, CA
Indiana National Bank, Boston, TX
International Data Group, Boston, MA
Kempner Insurance Company, New York, NY
King Investment Advisor, Inc, Houston, TX
Lang Communications, New York, NY
Library of Congress (Exit Art Reactions Exhibition), Washington, DC
Sidney Lewis Collection, Richmond, VA
Martin Margulies Collection, Miami, FL
Mayo Clinic, Rochester, MN
McDonalds Corporation, Oak Brook, IL
Mercer Company, New York, New York, NY
J. P. Morgan & Company, New York, New York, NY
Morgan Guarantee, New York, NY
New York Public Library, Lionel Pincus and Princess Firyal Map Collection, New York, NY
Nutter, McClennan & Fish, Boston, MA
Palm Hills Hotel, Okinawa, Japan
Peat, Marwich, Mitchell & Co, Montvale, NJ
Pew Charitable Trust, Philadelphia, Pa
Pfizer Pharmaceuticals, Inc, New York, NY
Polsinelli Collection, Los Angeles, CA
Prudential Life Insurance Company, Rockefeller Center, New York, NY
Quad Graphics, West Allis, IL
Quaker Oats, Chicago, IL
Randolph & Tate Associates, New York, NY

Reich & Tang, New York, NY
Simpson, Thacher, Bartlett, New York, NY
Skadden, Arps, Slate, Meagher & Flom, New York, NY
Solomon Equities, Inc, New York, NY
Tower Air, New York, NY
United States Department of State, Washington, DC
Vinson Elkins, Houston, TX
Wachovia, Charlotte, NC
E.M. Warburg Pincus, New York, NY
WFAE National Public Radio, Charlotte, NC
C. Wright Design, Mill Valley, CA
Zale Corporation, Dallas, TX
Zelle & Larson, St. Paul, MN

GRANTS

2016   Fulbright Senior Specialist Grant, India
2006   Visiting Artist Grant, Pang Mapha Highland Archaeology Project, Thailand
2003   Earthwork Installation Grant, Atlantic Flyway Project, Teaneck Creek Conservancy
2002   American Artists Abroad Grant, Art in Embassies Program, Riga, Latvia
       American Artists Abroad Grant, Art in Embassies Program, Tallinn, Estonia
       The Puffin Foundation Grant, paintings and photographs, Vietnam
2001   Visiting Artist Grant, United States, Bangkok, Thailand
1999   Pollock Krasner Foundation
1986   Pollock Krasner Foundation
1984   Ariana Foundation for the Arts
1983   Mid Atlantic States Consortium

TELEVISION FEATURES

2007   **Apsara Television,** June 9; feature of one-person exhibition at the Java Cafe Gallery, Phnom Penh, Cambodia
2005   Goodman, Janice; Feature, **WETA Public Television,** Around Town, Best Bets, August 5; feature of one-person exhibition at the National Academy of Sciences Gallery, Washington, DC
2001   **Television of Thailand,** Channel 11, July; feature of one-person exhibition at Silpakorn Gallery, Silpakorn University, Bangkok, Thailand

REVIEWS OF ONE-PERSON EXHIBITIONS

2008 "Mongolian Horses and Siberian Tigers- New Paintings on Paper and Canvas", **Absolutearts.com: Indepth Art News,** October 23; Review of one-person exhibition at Cheryl Pelavin Fine Arts, NYC; Color reproduction: *Crouching Tiger,* 2008

2007 Vachon, Michelle; "Back to Basics: Two Artists' Return to Drawing", **The Cambodia Daily,** Issue 483, June; Review of one-person exhibition at Java Cafe Gallery, Phnom Penh; Color reproductions: *Crossing the Street in Hanoi,* 1994 and *Resting Soldier,* 1994

Ledden, Liz; "Cambodian Journal: Human resilience and the strong Cambodian spirit are themes that artist Valentina DuBasky explores in her new exhibition", **Asia Life**; Review of one-person exhibition at Java Cafe Gallery, Phnom Penh

2006 Schwendener Martha; Review, **The New Yorker,** April 17; Review of one-person exhibition at Cheryl Pelavin Fine Arts, NYC

2005 LaFaso, Vanessa; "Larger Than Life: DuBasky's Oversize Work Focuses on Animal, Plant Life Along Silk Road", **The Washington Diplomat,** October; Review of one person exhibition at The National Academy of Sciences Gallery, Washington, DC; Color reproductions: *Gray Bird and Branches,* 2005, *Riverbirds, Fossils and Reeds,* 2005 and *Mountain Site,* 2003

Tierney, Robin; Review, **The Examiner,** October 29; Review of one-person exhibition at the National Academy of Sciences Gallery, Washington, DC; Color reproduction: *Red Bird & Reeds,* 2005

2001 Wilkinson, Jeanne C.; Review, **Tribeca Tribune,** Vol. 8, No. 4, December; Review of one-person exhibition at Cheryl Pelavin Fine Arts, NYC; Color reproduction: *Forest Site Wat Phimai,* 2001

"Ancient Futures: Cave-wall Landscape Paintings" **Bangkok Post,** June, 22; Review of one-person exhibition at Silpakorn Gallery, Silpakorn University, Bangkok, Thailand; Color reproduction: *Forest Site with Orchids & Bending Trees,* 2000

Review, **Naew Na,** June; Review of one-person exhibition at Silpakorn Gallery, Silpakorn University, Bangkok, Thailand

2000 Johnson, Ken; Review, **The New York Times,** February 4; Review of one-person exhibition at Cheryl Pelavin Fine Arts, NYC

Silverstein, Joel; **Review,** Review Magazine, January; Review of one-person exhibition at Cheryl Pelavin Fine Arts, NYC

Review, **Idaho Mountain Express,** Arts & Events, Sun Valley, Idaho, August 2; Review of one-person exhibition at Andria Friesen Fine Arts, Seattle; Color reproduction: *Forest Site with Spotted Stag,* 2000

Review, **Siam Rath,** June 21; Review of one-person exhibition at Silpakorn Gallery, Silpakorn University, Bangkok, Thailand

"New and Old", **The Nation,** July; Review of one-person exhibition at Silpakorn Gallery, Silpakorn University, Bangkok, Thailand; Color reproduction: *Forest Site with Orchids & Bending Trees,* 2000

"Ancient Futures", **Bangkok Post;** Review of one-person exhibition at Silpakorn Gallery, Silpakorn University, Bangkok, Thailand; Color reproductions: *Forest Site with Orchids & Bending Trees,* 2000 and *Forest Floor with Orchids,* 2000

"Ancient Futures: Cave-wall Landscape Paintings"; **Bangkok Post;** Review of one person exhibition at Silpakorn Gallery, Silpakorn University, Bangkok, Thailand; Color reproduction: *Forest Site with Stag & Bird,* 2000

1999 Henry, Gerrit; Review, **Art in America,** January; Review of one-person exhibition at Cheryl Pelavin Fine Arts, NYC; Color reproduction: *Syntax,* 1998

1997 Grau, Jane; Review, **Charlotte Newsstand,** Arts & Entertainment, November 1; Review of one-person exhibition at Hodges Taylor Gallery, Charlotte; Color reproduction: *Red Spotted Horse,* 1997

1991 Cohen, Ronny; Review, **Artforum,** December; Review of one-person exhibition at Ruth Siegel Gallery, NYC; Color reproduction: *Indonesia,* 1991

1986 Henry, Gerrit; Review, **Art in America,** April; Review of one-person exhibition at Oscarsson-Hood Gallery, NYC; Reproduction: *Primate,* 1986

Broelley, Doen; "Modern Day Cave Painting", **The Weekly,** Vol. 11, No. 25, June 18; Review of one-person exhibition at Hodges Banks Gallery, Seattle; Color reproduction: *Sienna Stag,* 1984

1985 Review, **Gallery Guide,** December; Review of one-person exhibition at Oscarsson Hood Gallery, NYC; Reproduction: *Rough Beast,* 1984

Harper, Paula; Review, **Miami News,** Miami Art Scene, April; One-person exhibition at Gloria Luria Gallery, Miami

Shanks, John Arthur; "Prehistory to Post Modernism", **Women Artists News,** Vol. 9, No. 2, Winter; Review of one-person exhibition at Semaphore Gallery, NYC; Reproduction: *Fallow Deer in Bracken,* 1983

1983 Zimmer, William; Review, **Arts Magazine;** Review of one-person exhibition at Oscarsson-Hood Gallery, NYC; Color reproduction: *Amber Stag,* 1983

1981 Parks, Addison; Review, **Arts Magazine,** Vol. 55, No. 6; Review of one-person exhibition at Semaphore Gallery, NYC; Color reproduction: *Split Cow,* 1981

Pellicone, William; Review, **Artspeak,** Vol. 2, No. 9; Review of one-person exhibition at Semaphore Gallery, NYC; Reproduction: *Split Cow,* 1981

Shanks, John Arthur; Review, **Women Artists News,** Winter/Spring; One-person exhibition at Semaphore Gallery, NYC; Color reproduction: *Split Cow,* 1981

FEATURE ARTICLES

2006 "Rain Clouds: Valentina DuBasky at Cheryl Pelavin Fine Arts", **The New York Sun,** On The Town, May 18; Color reproduction: *Riverbank Late Afternoon,* 2006

2003 Gomez, Edward M.; "Reimagining the Landscape: Contemporary Painters Bring Fresh Ideas and Techniques to a Classic Art Form", **Art & Antiques**, Vol. 26, No. 10, October; Color reproduction: *Open Forest,* 2001

Cebere, Gundega; "Amerikas Maksla Riga", **Maksla Plus: Kulturas Zurnals,** Vol. 1, No. 33, February/March; Color reproductions: *Heron,* 1995, and *Heron, Warbler and Milkweed,* 1991

Ash, Elizabeth; "The Art of Visual Diplomacy", **State Magazine,** No. 464, January

2002 Osadchaja, Irina; "Old Birds Under One Roof" **Architecture and Design in the Baltics,** No. 5, Riga, Latvia, October; Color reproductions: *Heron,* 1995, and *Heron, Warbler and Milkweed,* 1991

"In the News: Artist and Their Art Go Abroad", **State Magazine,** No. 463, December; Color reproduction: *Heron, Warbler and Milkweed,* 1991

2000 Bailey, Susan; "Western Explorers Meet Explorations on Canvas and Film", **Seattle Wood River Journal,** August 2; 2000; Color reproduction: *Forest Site with River & Orchids,* 2000

Stasz, Meagan; "Painting Profile: Modern Landscape Painting", **Sun Valley Art,** Vol. 6, Nos. 8 & 9, February-March; Color reproductions: *Forest Site with Orchids & Wild Grass,* 2000 and *Forest Canopy & Botanicas,* 2000

1986 Cohrs, Timothy; "Hudson River Editions, Pelavin Editions-A Report Back from the Other World of Printmaking", **Arts Magazine,** November; Color reproduction: *Stag/Red Meander,* 1985

REVIEWS OF GROUP EXHIBITIONS

2001 Shaw, Kurt; "Pair of Shows Comment on Environmental Issues Facing Our Nation and the World", **Tribune,** Review, November 16

1988 Ahlander, Leslie Judd; "Sculpture is the focus of Gallery Show", **The Miami News,** June 3; Reproduction: *Standing Camel,* 1988

1985 Cecil, Sarah; "Group Show: Wolff Gallery", **ARTnews,** January

1983 Miro, Marsha; Review, **Detroit Free Press,** November
Review, **Detroit News,** November

1981 Review, **Where Magazine,** August

1980 Larsen, Kay; "Reports from the Front", **The Village Voice,** Vol. 25, No. 7
Rickey, Carrie; Review, **The Village Voice**

REPRODUCTIONS OF PAINTINGS IN PUBLICATIONS

2017 **International Journal of Visual Arts,** Studies and Communication, Volume 20; Number 20; publisher Dr. Shekhar Chandra Joshi, Almora, Uttarakhand, India; Front and back cover color reproductions: *Stag in Blue Field,* 2014, *Kali/ Black Madonna,* 1998 and *Valley of Flowers,* 2015

2015 Walsh, Mary; **Kinetiv: Highlights from the Polsinelli Art Collection;** Color reproduction: *Amber Birds with Indigo Mountain,* 2013

2010 Hayes, Linda; "Tall Order", **Luxe Magazine:** Interiors + Design Pacific Northwest Edition, Issue 1, Vol. 8, Winter; Color reproduction: *River Fragments Grey Bird,* 1990

2006 **The Lakeville Journal,** August 10; Reproduction: *Eurasian Steppe Horse,* 2004

2005 **The National Academies Press,** Trade Offerings; publisher Joseph Henry Press, Color reproduction: *Cranes, Warblers and Ironwood,* 2003

2005 **The National Academies Press,** New and Forthcoming Books, publisher Joseph Henry Press; Color reproduction: *Shore Site,* 2005

2002 Seely, Christopher; **Southern Voice,** October 11; Color reproduction: *Yellow Bird in Grey Field,* 2002

2000 **Idaho Mountain Express,** August 2; Color reproduction: *Forest Site with Spotted Stag,* 2000

1999 **The Sciences Magazine,** July/August; Color reproduction: *Pond Site,* 1999

1997 **Carolina Arts,** Vol. 1, No. 9; Color reproduction: *Red Spotted Horse,* 1997
Southern Accents, Charlotte; Color reproduction: *Red Horse/ Split,* 1997

1992 **Christian Science Monitor,** November 23; Color reproduction: *Heron Cove,* 1990

1991 **The Menniger Perspective,** Issue No. 3; Color reproduction: *Eastern Quarter,* 1991

1990 **Ms Magazine,** poster publication; Color reproduction: *Heron Cove,* 1990

1988 **The Pollock Krasner Foundation Annual Report;** Reproduction: *Strata,* 1984
Legacy Foundation; Color reproduction: *Good Medicine,* monoprint, 1996

1985 "The Ancestor that Wasn't", **The Sciences Magazine,** March/April; Color reproduction: *Back to Back,* 1984

1983 **The Newark Museum Annual Report,** Reproduction: *Bucks Country,* 1983

1980 **Maenad Magazine,** Reproduction: *Spotted Bison,* and four paintings, 1980

REVIEWS OF FINE ART PRINTS

2020 O'Shaughnessy, Tracey; "Celebration of a Unique Singularity: Monoprint Show Featured", **REP/Republican American,** June 13

2014 "Selected New Editions", **Art in Print,** March-April; Color reproduction: *Cliff Site with Red Heron,* monoprint, 2013

"New Editions", **Journal of the Print World,** April/May/June; Color reproduction: *Amber Birds with Indigo Mountain,* monoprint, 2013

2001 Szeto-Chan, Erin; Review, **In New York**, Eclectic Collector, July; Color reproduction: *Tiger Orchid/ Sri Lanka,* monoprint, 2001

1992 Marimo, Meri; Review, **Twenty-First Century Prints,** August; Color reproduction: *River Edge,* monoprint, 1990

1988 Review, **Print News: International Journal of Contemporary Prints,** Vol. 8, No. 2, Spring; Color reproduction: *Ragtime Hart,* monoprint,1985

1986 Beller, Tom; "Ancient Art Comes Alive" **West Side Spirit,** Arts & Entertainment, July 14; Color reproductions: *Leaping Brindled Stag,* 1984 and *Ragtime Hart,* 1984

1984 Cohen, Ronny; "New Editions", **ARTnews,** April; Color reproduction: *Dune Horse/ Starry Night,* lithograph, 1984
Review, **The Print Collectors Newsletter,** Vol. 15, No. 3, July-August; Color reproductions: *Claret Stag in Plum Field,* 1984 and *Leaping Brindled Stag,* 1984

1983 Review, **The Print Collectors Newsletter,** Vol. 14, No. 5; Color reproduction: *Dune Horse/Starry Night,* 1983

ESSAYS IN CATALOGS

2019 Ambassador Branstad, Terry; **United States Embassy Beijing: Art in Embassies Exhibition;** Color reproductions: *Yellow Crane and Moon,* 2017, *Herons, Warblers and Reed Grass,* 2017, and *Riverbirds, Fossils and Reeds,* 2005

2017 Goodman, Jonathan; **The Trace,** Lichtundfire Gallery; Color reproduction: *Bison*

2016 **The Journey of the Red Horse:** Horse and Stag Paintings by Valentina DuBasky, Published by Abingdon Square Publishing; Color reproductions: Cover and 13 color plates

2014 **Tandem Press:** fine contemporary prints, fall, 2014, Published by Tandem Press Color reproductions: Monotypes and lithograph by Valentina DuBasky, 15 color plates, centerfold, pages 15-23

2008 Shoocongdej, Rasmi; **From [Different] Horizons of Rockshelter;** publisher Silpakorn University Press, Bangkok, Thailand; Color reproductions: 6 paintings from the Pang Mapha Highland Archaeology Project

2005 Nadelman, Cynthia, essay; Talasak, J.D.; introduction; **Riverbirds and Rainforests,** National Academy of Sciences Gallery, publisher The National Academies of Sciences, Washington, DC; Color reproductions: 11 color plates

2003 Ambassador Watt, Linda E; **United States Embassy Panama:** Art in Embassies Exhibition; Color reproductions: *Untitled,* 1998, *Shore Site,* 1991 and *Rainforest,* 1999

2002 Ambassador Carlson, Brian E.; **Art in Embassies Exhibition at the Residence of the American Ambassador Riga**; Color reproductions: *Heron, Warbler and Milkweed,* 1991 (cover) and *Heron,* 1995

Toxic Landscapes: Artists Examine the Environment, Printed by the Puffin Foundation; Reproduction: Tragic Harvest, 1991, p20

2001 Henry, Gerrit; **Forests, Orchids & Fossils;** Color reproductions: 9 color plates

1999 **Oil & Wax: Chapter & Verse;** Color Reproduction: *Spotted Horse,* 1999

1998 **American Artists at American Ambassador's Residence - Muscat, Sultanate of Oman;** Essay by US Ambassador Frances D. Cook; Printed by US Department of State; Color Reproduction: Heron Cove, 1990, p14

1990 Hartney, Eleanor and Hanson, Trudy; **Presswork: the Art of Women Printmakers,** Lang Publications; Color reproduction: *Heron Cove,* 1990

1987 **Rutgers Archives for Printmaking Studios, Catalog of Acquisitions,** 1985
1987, Jane Voorhees Zimmerli Art Museum, Rutgers University; Reproductions: *Red Stag Diptych,*1984, *Leaping Brindled Stag,* 1984, *Claret Stag in Plum Field,* 1984, *Small Stag Series,* 1984, and *Gray Stag/ Ochre Field,* 1984

1985 Raynor, Vivian; **Intaglio Printing in the 1980's; Jane Voorhees Zimmerli Art Museum**

1984 Gustafon, Donna; **Surface Printing in the 1980's; Lithographs, Screenprints & Monoprints from the Rutgers Archives for Printmaking Studios,** Jane Voorhees Zimmerli Art Museum, Rutgers University; Reproduction: *Gray Stag/Ochre Field,* 1984

1981 **The Working Process;** Color Reproduction: *Untitled*, 1981
Browning, Robert; **Mixed Bag,** printed by the Alternative Museum, 1981 | Reproduction: *Cumulus on the Mount,* 1981, p12

BOOK PUBLICATIONS

2020 DuBasky, Valentina; **Horned and Antlered Animals;** Abingdon Square Publishing

2019 Kernan, Catherine and Rooney, E. Ashley, with Einstein, Laura G. and Oresman, Janice C; **Singular & Series: Contemporary Monotype and Monoprint;** Schiffer Publishing

2009 DuBasky, Valentina; **The Cambodian Journal: Drawings 1994-1998;** Abingdon Square Publishing

FINE ART PRINT PUBLICATIONS

2013 Tandem Press
1984-2008 Pelavin Editions, Ltd
1983 Solo Press

List of Plates

White Addax with Magenta Horns	2020	Oil on canvas	11 x 14 inches	page 5
Spotted Goat	2020	Oil on canvas	11 x 14 inches	page 7
Markhor	2020	Oil on paper	20 x 24 inches	page 9
Spotted Goat in Red Field	2018	Oil on canvas	22 x 30 inches	page 11
Himalayan Antelope with Spiral Horns	2019	Oil on canvas	14 x 11 inches	page 13
White Ram with Spiral Horns	2020	Oil on canvas	14 x 11 inches	page 15
Recumbent Bull with Blue Horns	2020	Oil on canvas	14 x 11 inches	page 17
Bison	2017	Acrylic on plaster and paper	30.5 x 33 inches	page 19
White Bison with Ochre Markings	2020	Oil on canvas	12 x 16 inches	page 21
Spotted Goat	2020	Oil on canvas	16 x 20 inches	page 23
Spiral Horned Goat	2020	Oil on paper	22 x 30 inches	page 25
Tricolor Bison	2020	Oil on paper	14.75 x 20 inches	page 27
Turning Stag with Rose Antlers	2020	Oil on paper	22 x 30 inches	page 29
Red and White Antlered Stag	2020	Oil on canvas	12 x 16 inches	page 31
Addax in Blue Field	2019	Oil on canvas	14 x 11 inches	page 33
Blue Marsh Deer with Branching Antlers	2019	Oil on canvas	14 x 11 inches	page 35
Rose Antlered Forest Deer	2019	Oil on canvas	14 x 11 inches	page 37
White Spotted Bison	2020	Oil on canvas	14 x 11 inches	page 39
Lyre Horned Bison	2020	Oil on canvas	12 x 16 inches	page 41
Athenian Goat	2018	Oil on canvas	22 x 30 inches	page 43
Blue Antlered Temple Deer	2020	Oil on paper	22 x 30 inches	page 45
Gray Spotted Antelope in Magenta Field	2020	Oil on canvas	12 x 16 inches	page 47
Goat with Fluted Horns	2019	Oil on canvas	14 x 11 inches	page 49
White Speckled Antelope in Magenta Field	2020	Oil on canvas	14 x 11 inches	page 51
Red Antlered Stag	2020	Oil on paper	11 x 14 inches	page 53
Split Stag in Red Field	2018	Oil on canvas	30 x 22 inches	page 55
Red Goat in Ochre Field	2014	Monotype	10 x 8 inches	page 59
Tien Shan Goat	2014	Monotype	10 x 8 inches	page 61
Himalayan Goat	2018	Monotype and chine-collé	8 x 10 inches	page 63
Blue Stag	2014	Monotype	10 x 8 inches	page 65

www.ingramcontent.com/pod-product-compliance
Lightning Source LLC
Chambersburg PA
CBHW042320210526

45473CB00007B/2400